THE FOUR CARDINAL PRINCIPLES OF TRADING

THE FOUR CARDINAL PRINCIPLES OF TRADING

How the World's Top Traders Identify Trends, Cut Losses, Maximize Profits & Manage Risk

BRUCE BABCOCK

IRWIN
Professional Publishing®
Chicago • London • Singapore

Times Mirror
Higher Education Group

Library of Congress Cataloging-in-Publication Data

Babcock, Bruce.
    The four cardinal principles of trading : how the world's top traders identify trends, cut losses, maximize profits, and manage risk / Bruce Babcock.
        p.   cm.
    Includes bibliographical references and index.
    ISBN 0-7863-1010-3
    1. Commodity exchanges–United States.   2. Commodity futures.
    I. Title.
    HG6049.B33   1996
    332.63'28–dc20   96–2062

Printed in the United States of America
1 2 3 4 5 6 7 8 9 BS 0 3 2 1 0 9 8 7 6

*To Larry Regg, who for many
years has helped me get to the
place where I could write this book*

CONTENTS

Chapter 3

Cut Losses Short   71

Chapter 4

Let Profits Run   110

Chapter 5

Manage Risk   143

Chapter 6

Psychology   207

Chapter 7

Summary and Conclusion   212

CHAPTER 1

Introduction

Profitable commodity trading is one of the most difficult endeavors known to man. It must be, as so few are able to achieve success at it. When I first started trading over 20 years ago, there was a dearth of information about how to trade properly. There were only a few books, half a dozen advisory letters, and several chart services. Mechanical trading systems were virtually unknown. There were no personal computers.

In the last 20 years, hundreds of books have been published. Personal computers have been invented, and their cost has dropped to make them available to everyone with the capital to trade. Thousands of computer software programs have been created to assist traders. Trading systems have gone from a curiosity to commonplace. It used to be that primitive, futile trading systems were advertised and sold for thousands of dollars. If you wanted to test your own trading ideas on a computer, you had to learn how to program yourself or pay high fees for custom programming. Now traders with no programming ability can buy software for a few hundred dollars that enables them to create, test, and trade their own mechanical systems.

You would think that this avalanche of information and assistance would make it easier to trade correctly and profitably. Not so. Much of what has been published is simply wrong. It is not easy to separate the good from the bad in futures trading literature. Even well-received books by respected authors are full of useless ideas that don't work. The only way to be sure your trading ideas really make money is to conduct rigorous historical testing, preferably on a computer that doesn't make mistakes. You must also understand the testing process because even computer testing can be misleading if you don't know what you are doing.

Another substantial barrier to profitable trading is the human mind. Even when people know how to trade correctly, it is still very difficult actually to do it. Our human emotions constantly tempt us to violate the principles we know to be correct.

In an effort to achieve perfection, traders constantly strive to complicate the trading problem. Yet experience has shown this doesn't help. Simple trading approaches are invariably superior to anything you can invent using calculus and complicated equations.

In spite of outward appearances, successful trading is not intellectually difficult. One of my favorite commodity quotes is from Richard Dennis, perhaps the first really big trading success (he made hundreds of millions of dollars in the early 1980s): "Commodity trading is a lot less complicated than meets the eye."

I believe you can reduce successful trading to four key principles, which are the basis of this book:

1. Trade with the trend.
2. Cut losses short.
3. Let profits run.
4. Manage risk.

I cannot imagine any successful trading approach that does not incorporate each of these principles in some way.

While almost everyone pays lip service to these concepts, almost no one actually implements them correctly in their trading. This may be because while they know the principle, they don't know what it means. Or they may think they are applying the correctly understood principle when in reality they are not. Or they may rationalize that a particular principle is not important in their unique situation.

Another reality of trading is that there are different ways to implement the principles correctly. As Jack Schwager said in *The New Market Wizards:* "There are a million ways to make money in the markets. The irony is that they are all very difficult to find."

In an effort to help traders understand the four key principles and at the same time see different ways to implement them, I interviewed a number of trading experts I have come to know as editor and publisher of *Commodity Traders Consumer Report*. Each of them trades for his or her own account. I asked each one how important each principle was in his or her own trading and specifically how it was implemented. These interviews originally appeared in five installments in *CTCR*. I have re-edited and expanded the material for this book. I have also included here substantial parts of the interviews that for space reasons I was unable to fit in *CTCR*.

I asked each expert about the theory and practical application of the principles. Everyone seems to have his or her own interpretation of these axioms and the procedures for implementing them. The result is a broad cross-section of opinions and trading ideas that are bound to provide great food for thought in helping you create a complete trading plan for yourself.

I did not interview Courtney Smith as part of the project. However, I have included his comments on risk management in this book. They came from a separate interview I did of Courtney for a previous *CTCR* cover story.

I have presented the four key concepts in the order most people generally list and discuss them. This does not imply any hierarchy of importance. As you will see, there are differences of opinion about that as well.

Since I assume you already have a basic knowledge of commodity trading, there is no need for any further introduction. In the next chapter, we'll get right to the first cardinal principle. I start with the concept that is most basic to the trade selection process.

CHAPTER 2

Trade with the Trend

■ have argued for many years that because of the nature of markets, to be successful trading commodities, you must trade with the trend. Mathematical analysis has shown that in most commodity markets price action is primarily random with a small trend component. It is the trend component that allows a trader to achieve a long-term statistical edge that translates into profits. If there were no trend component, everyone would eventually lose because the costs of trading would overcome any random short-term profits. In order to exploit the trend component, however, you must trade with the trend.

Trend is only relevant in a particular time frame. The shorter the time frame, the more difficult it is to obtain a statistical edge. This is because short-term price action is the most random and because the shorter the time frame, the greater the costs of trading become as a percentage of the return on the average trade.

I assert that those who consider themselves "countertrend" traders are really trend traders in a shorter time frame. They also tend to anticipate rather than wait for a confirmation of trend change. This is a matter of semantics rather than trading wisdom, however.

The key issues are whether you know what your trading time frame is, whether you have a specific means of identifying the trend in that time frame, and whether you apply your rules consistently. For help in considering these questions, I turn to some friends of mine, all of whom are experienced professional traders. Biographies appear in this chapter along with their comments.

RISK-SELECTED TREND TIME FRAME

Two people with whom I spoke advocated trend selection as a part of the money management process rather than just for creating entry rules: Steve Briese and Jake Bernstein.

Steve Briese

Steve, what is your concept of trading with the trend?

Trading with the trend is a truism. Nobody intentionally trades against the trend. You lose money trading against the trend. The critical factor is identifying which trend you intend to trade. You might trade the hourly or daily or weekly or a very long-term trend. Then you select your indicators based on that trend.

For instance, if you're trading an hourly trend, you don't take your entry points or stop-loss points from monthly charts. Determining that length of trend is inextricably tied to the other three principles: cutting losses, letting profits run, and managing risk. If you don't identify which trend you're trading, you can't accomplish any of those.

If somebody is trying to identify what trend they want to trade, how do they go about doing that?

Other than trader preference, the selection of the trend is often dictated by account size. If you begin with the idea that you want to manage risk by limiting the potential loss on any one trade to a percentage of your account size, that would affect the time frame you choose to trade. You could start looking at monthly charts and determining entry points through standard chart formations. You could decide where the stop-loss point would have to be to justify that trade based on standard chart trading techniques. Using monthly charts, you may well find the amount of loss to be too high a percentage of your account to accommodate your risk management rule. Therefore, you couldn't trade such a long-term trend. Most traders end up on daily charts as a maximum.

Each chart pattern has an objective and a stop-loss point where you know that the chart pattern has failed. That is the point at which you must exit your losing trade. You have to determine the size of the chart patterns you can

Steve Briese

Steve Briese is editor and publisher of the *Bullish Review of Commodity Futures Markets* newsletter. Published biweekly since 1988, it reports on and analyzes the data in the *CFTC Commitments of Traders Reports*.

Briese, now 46 years old, retired from his successful home construction business on his 40th birthday to pursue his futures trading interests. He trades for his own account as well as publishing his newsletter, systems, and software for traders.

In addition to writing about trading, Briese is also an accomplished computer programmer. He has been programming since the personal computer started to become popular in the early 1980s. He has created a number of unique and successful software programs for traders. He is currently working on a Windows version of *Autopilot*, a charting program. He also sells two system programs: *Cross-Current* is a currency spread trading system and *Private $tock* is for stock futures.

You can write to Steve at Bullish Review, 14600 Blaine Avenue East, Rosemount, MN 55068. Phone: (612)-423-4900. Fax (612)-423-4949.

trade based on what the projected entry and stop would be and relate that to your account size. How long a trend to trade is based on how big that loss is in relation to your account.

What you seem to be saying is you can't determine the real trend that you're trading until you see what your entry and stop are?

That's right.

If that's so, you couldn't include a trend indicator with your trade selection filters because you wouldn't know what length to use.

As a practical matter, if you're just getting started, identification of what trend you're going to trade is the first priority. You look at various methods and systems and see where typical entries, exits, and risks are.

Every system trades some sort of trend. How they enter with that trend can vary, but every system is designed to trade some sort of trend. You can see by the history of the system what the average risk is. If the risk is such that you're not risking more than 5 percent of your account (and preferably only one to 2 percent of your account), that's the length of trend you should be trading.

Do you then use some sort of trend indicator as an entry filter?

Entry into the trend is a separate matter. Let me use chart-based trading as an example since nearly everyone starts there. Assume a triangular chart pattern and that you'll be going long on an upside breakout. You can identify where your stop-loss should be. It will be the point below the triangle where you could say the triangle pattern had failed.

If that projected potential loss is too large a percentage of your account, there are only two things you can do: (1) pass the trade entirely or (2) wait for a better entry. You can't change the stop. You've already determined the stop based on where you know the trend will have turned against you. So you must adjust your entry or pass the trade.

A breakout-type entry often entails too much risk. Another method is to anticipate the breakout and enter at a price that keeps your risk to a reasonable percentage of your account. In our example you might enter while price is still within the triangle, possibly even close to the lower end of the triangle, where your risk is going to be smaller because your stop-loss is going to be closer. That's a method you can use to trade a longer-term trend than you could otherwise afford to trade.

Beginning traders who start with $5,000 or $10,000 accounts can't really afford to trade standard patterns on daily charts in the accepted manner. The solution is to find a way to anticipate, either by anticipating the pattern the chart will complete or using oscillators to buy on weakness or sell on strength.

What about using standard entries and adjusting your risk with money management stops?

That's not the best way to set a stop. You're not waiting for your trend to reverse itself before abandoning the trade. I find myself in this kind of predicament all the time because I'm not willing to risk more than $500 per contract on a trade regardless of my account size. In order to respect that limit, I set the stop point first. Then my entry point can be no more than $500 above the stop point (for longs).

I'm buying as the market is coming to me. The short-term trend has not fully established itself. I count on other factors to make that trend turn up. One of those other factors is the next longer-term trend. The longer-term trend should have an effect on a market. When the short-term trend becomes oversold, the longer-term trend will move the shorter trend back up. You can use different length oscillators to measure the longer-term trend.

Another indicator I favor is the Commitments of Traders data, which I analyze in my newsletter. In a sustained uptrend, a reaction will often run its course when prices react back to a point where commercials start aggressive accumulation. When I see this accumulation, it is a confirmation that the major trend is about to reassert itself.

When you say you look at the next longer-term trend to see if it's in line with the trade, how do you determine what the next longer-term trend is?

I go from a daily chart to a weekly chart.

How do you determine what the trend is on a weekly chart?

You can use trendlines, or the longer-term oscillators shown with the commercial weekly charts, or regression (the best-fit line). There are many methods to determine trend. You can draw a trendline under the lows or above the highs to see what direction prices are going.

If your trendline points down, you assume the trend is down and vice versa?

Yes. One tool that I use that isn't available anyplace else other than in my own charting software package is moving average trading bands. J.D. Hearst wrote a book about these back in the early 1970s called *The Profit Magic of Stock Transaction Timing*. My trading bands are similar to his except that they are fixed in height.

Jake Bernstein

Another expert who incorporates trend selection into the risk management process is Jake Bernstein.

Jake, where does trading with the trend fit into your approach?

Of all the common market principles, I put "trade with the trend" at the very top. It's a lesson I've had to learn and relearn practically every year. All traders have the tools to find trends. That's what makes it especially frustrating when we go contrary to the trend or when we try to pick tops and bottoms. I would add to the principle of determining the trend, if the trend is up, buy at support and if the trend is down, sell at resistance. If traders could do just those simple things, they would (*a*) stay out of trouble and (*b*) make money. That's the bottom line.

When you talk about trading with the trend, how do you define the trend?

The trend is relative to the trader's time frame. A five-minute uptrend in bonds may be a lifetime to a floor trader, whereas it's totally meaningless to a longer-term trader working in a bank.

You have the intraday trend, daily trend, weekly trend, monthly trend, and yearly trend. It's not possible for a trader to trade all trends or even to determine all trends at once. To attempt that would be to invite total confusion.

A trader must pick a meaningful trend length for him. Do you have any guidelines for people as to how they might do that?

That part is all psychological. Through experience or trial and error each trader has to find the time frame within which he or she is comfortable. I'm reminded of a story in *Reminiscences of a Stock Market Operator* where a man came to Jesse Livermore and told him he was long a great deal of stock and was having trouble sleeping. He asked what to do. Livermore said, "You've got to sell down to the sleeping level." Finding the right time frame for your trades is very much like that. You have to find out which time frame causes you the least anxiety. In having the least anxiety, you're going to make the fewest emotional decisions.

Jake Bernstein

Jake Bernstein is an internationally recognized futures analyst, trader, and author. He has written more than 25 books on futures trading, stock trading, trader psychology, and economic forecasting. Bernstein is publisher of the *MBH Weekly Futures Trading Letter,* which has been in continuous publication since 1972. With over 20 years of trading experience, Jake has lived through all types of markets and has tested and traded literally hundreds of trading systems. His expertise is in the area of seasonality, cycles, timing methods, trading systems, economic forecasting, and market patterns.

Jake has appeared regularly on national radio and television and has been a guest on *Wall Street Week.* His forecasts and opinions are quoted frequently in the financial press the world over. He is a much sought after speaker at financial and investment conferences.

As a former clinical psychologist, Jake has developed a keen understanding of trader behavior. He brings his understandings of human nature and trader psychology to his technical work as a market analyst and trader.

In addition to his expertise in trader psychology, Jake has pioneered numerous technical and seasonal methodologies in the futures markets, including the following: Key Date Seasonal Analysis, the Daily Sentiment Indicator, the MAC trading method, the Stochastic Pop Indicator, numerous market patterns, and a variety of short-term and intermediate-term trading systems including the Critical Time of Day system, which is a method designed exclusively for day-trading.

Among Jake's more well-known books are *The Investor's Quotient, Seasonal Concepts in Futures Trading, The New Investor's Quotient, Market Masters, Why Traders Lose—How Traders Win, The Handbook of Commodity Cycles, The Handbook of Economic Cycles,* and his latest, *Seasonal Trader's Bible.* He has also published a number of unique systems and software programs.

You may write Jake at MBH, P.O. Box 353, Winnetka, IL 60093. Call (708)-291-1870.

How would you recommend a beginner start out?

There are many good seasonal patterns or short-term patterns that run anywhere from 5 to 20 days. I think psychologically these are the most tolerable for most traders. Given the natural tendency for traders to cut profits short and let losses run, trading a shorter-term time frame helps you overcome those harmful impulses.

Some of the research I've done in the last year has shown a distinct tendency for markets to change direction about every 14 days. There's a tendency to move higher for about 14 trading days in an uptrend—not higher every single day, of course—and then have a correction that usually lasts about 4 to 6 days. It's during those little corrections that most traders get stopped or scared out. Psychologically, if you set yourself up to trade within those time frames, you're much better off.

Let's talk about some trend indicators that you use. Which ones do you like? For what time frames?

I used to like a lot of them. In my old age I have learned to keep it simple. Within virtually all time frames, the little technique I use seems to answer most of the important questions about trading. Those questions are: (*a*) where is the trend, (*b*) where is support, and (*c*) where is resistance. My favorite indicator consists of a moving average channel composed of a 10-bar moving average of the highs and an 8-bar moving average of the lows.

How does your high/low channel indicator measure trend?

The trend turns up when you have two successive price bars completely above the top moving average. It remains up until you have two successive price bars completely below the bottom moving average. It's not perfect. But it is a very mechanical—and I can't stress *mechanical* enough—method for determining the trend.

When the trend is up, if you're in the market, you're only going to be long, and when the trend is down, you're only going to be short?

That's right.

Do you have some other little tips on trend trading?

If you're a very short-term trader, buy lower opens in an uptrend and sell higher opens in a downtrend. You can exit those positions on the close.

Another important relationship that has persisted for many years is the relationship between the open and the close. In uptrending markets the closes tend to be higher than the opens. In downtrending markets the closes tend to be lower than the opens.

Another little pattern I like consists of three successive price bars that each shows higher highs, higher lows, and higher closes. When you get three such successive price bars, you have confirmation that the trend is up, that there is accumulation. The reverse pattern applies to downtrends.

LONG-TERM TRADERS

Nick Van Nice

The longest term trend-follower I interviewed was Nick Van Nice.

Nick, how important do you think trading with the trend is to successful trading?

Trading with the trend is very important to successful trading. I like to trade with mature trends that are nine months or older in duration. I define my trends using the Dow Theory. That means a series of higher intermediate-term highs and higher intermediate-term lows (for uptrends). I generally won't trade a market unless it shows a clear pattern like that for at least nine months. Trends of that time frame in that pattern are one of the few things that hold up over time and that exhibit probabilities that make them worth trading. The flip side is my observation that a corrective movement is very random and nearly impossible to capture.

Nine months seems awfully long to wait for a trend to establish itself. How did you get to that long a period?

I found that transitional time frames, where you go from a long-term uptrend to a long-term downtrend, may last from six to nine months. During

Nick Van Nice

Nick Van Nice has been tracking the commodity markets since the late 1970s. He grew up on a farm near Davenport, Iowa, and was born into a family of very successful traders. The Van Nices raised a variety of grains and used the markets for hedging. That eventually led to speculation.

Nick is a third-generation trader. His grandfather, James Van Nice, began trading wheat futures back in the 1920s. Nick's father, Joe Van Nice, founded Commodity Trend Service, a leading chart service publisher. Nick has inherited his father's mantle and his market insights are now published each week in *Futures Charts* and have been broadcast each Monday morning on CNBC since August 1993. Reuters News Service, the worlds largest electronic publisher, also distributes Nick's commentary.

In the summer of 1993, Nick addressed the prestigious Canadian Society of Technical Analysts at the Toronto Stock Exchange, and he explained his many successful trading techniques at the National Introducing Brokers Association in Chicago in June 1994. He is currently an active member of the Market Technicians Association and is a regular contributing writer for *Agri-Finance Magazine*.

Write Nick at Commodity Trend Service, P.O. Box 32309, Palm Beach Gardens, FL 33420. Phone (800)-331-1069 or (407)-694-0960.

that period prices are very choppy and almost impossible to trade. So I have elected to give up those first nine months. I won't trade it until I've already seen nine months of trend. Going back to the Dow Theory, I like to have at least three higher highs and three higher lows in the pattern.

Do you look at weekly, daily, or monthly charts?

I spot the trend on weekly charts.

If you're waiting nine months for the trend to get started, how long is the average long-term trend you're trying to trade?

The trends I'm looking for are between three and five years long. We've been in a down market in commodities since the early 1980s. Those are the kinds of trends I'm looking for. Very long-term moves. All I'm interested in is the middle of these big trends.

I realize that sometimes I sacrifice good trending moves—like the bonds right now [spring 1994]. Most everybody is short bonds. My system won't let me trade yet. To me that's okay because there are plenty of other opportunities out there.

Wouldn't you still be trying to go long bonds?

Exactly. If my model would give buy signals, I would be on the long side.

If you require nine months for a trend to be established, that means that in the first nine months of a downtrend you're buying. Isn't that true?

I'll tell you how I do it. I have criteria on how much correction is required. Then I simply use a four-week breakout rule as an intermediate-term filter for my trades. It works quite nicely.

I'm not always in the market. Lots of times I'm just sitting. My intermediate-term bond indicator is still down. As soon as we get a four-week breakout to the upside in the bonds, I'll be looking for my entry trigger to get long. The trigger is a simple moving average system.

That takes tremendous discipline, but your testing and experience indicate it is the way to go?

The initial tests I've done show that it's more profitable than our *Trendsetter* system [tracked in the *CTCR* centerfold]. I'm actually trading it for the *Candlestick Hotline*, although it has nothing to do with candlesticks. We're up about 20 percent for the year so far, which is pretty good.

It certainly keeps you from picking tops and bottoms, doesn't it?

It really does, and that's the key. I'll let everybody else beat themselves up trying to be smarter and quicker.

Bob Jubb

Another relatively long-term trader is Bob Jubb.

Bob, is trading with the trend important in your methodology?

I find trading with the trend to be one of the keys to success, no question. If you get a hold of a few trends, you don't need anything else. Even one good trend that lasts more than a year is all anyone would probably need for that year. If you try to fight a trend, you can get stopped out over and over. It's better to switch to the other side or find another market.

Over the last 20 years I have experienced an average of three to four good trends a year and found myself wrong maybe three or four times a year max. If you catch one trend, that makes up for lots of losses.

The secret is if you can catch just the middle part of a trend, you can make a lot of money. Searching for the absolute bottom or a top, you can get burned many times. By the time it finally does bottom, you'll be disappointed in your failures and looking elsewhere. I try to find the middle half of a trend rather than a top or a bottom.

Before you initiate a trade, how do you determine what the trend is in a market?

With seasonality. I always start with seasonal charts. They help find trends that are just beginning.

Whose seasonal charts do you use?

Shearson's.

What about markets that don't have seasonal charts?

I usually avoid them.

Bob Jubb

Bob Jubb has been immersed in markets since the age of 11. At that young age his great uncle introduced him to the art of charting as well as how to buy and sell common stocks.

During the 1960s, he studied the Elliott Wave Theory and the Wyckoff Method. As a college student he began managing funds as well as writing a small investment newsletter for friends.

After graduating from Michigan State University with a degree in finance, Jubb worked as an accountant for a CPA firm for one year. He then joined an NYSE regional brokerage firm as a research analyst. He specialized in auto and related stocks.

In 1974, he left to start his own mergers and acquisitions firm. He closed that in 1975 to devote full time to developing the three newsletters his company, Techno-Fundamental Investments, Inc., has been publishing ever since: *Tomorrow's Stocks*, *Tomorrow's Options,* and *Tomorrow's Commodities.*

In the 1950s investment research was primarily oriented towards fundamentals. Technical research became more popular in the 1960s. Jubb combined both technical and fundamental research methods in an effort to develop a consistently efficient research approach for investing in stocks, commodities, and options.

To further meet the needs of his subscribers, in January 1986, TFI began offering the TFI Personal Advisory Line. Through this vehicle TFI can provide its customers not only with a variety of newsletters, but also personal guidance and management of their investment portfolios.

Bob Jubb is now 48 years old, married, with three children. They reside in Scottsdale, Arizona.

You can contact him at TFI, Inc., P.O. Box 14111, Scottsdale, AZ 85267. Telephone (602)-996-2908.

You compare daily charts with seasonal charts to find those that seem to be lining up. Those are your trade candidates?

Right.

Which major markets don't have seasonality?

Most of the financials.

The currencies?

Bonds do. Currencies are nowhere near as good as something that grows.

Gold, silver, stocks, and bonds don't grow.

No, but they're affected by the calendar, such as a year-end effect. Silver is affected by industrial demand, so you have the winter slowdown.

How long would a daily chart trend have to be established in the direction of the seasonal trend before you would be willing to say that the trend was in conjunction?

Usually four weeks. I like to see a month.

Once you have a qualifying trade candidate, how do you enter in the direction of the trend?

I usually just buy the open. Another important ingredient to a trade for me is a two-to-one reward/risk ratio.

You don't have any fancy entry methods or filters. You see a trade opportunity, and you go in.

Yes.

Yet you've been very successful. It just shows if you trade with the

trend, you don't need a fancy entry system. That is contrary to what most traders are doing. They're spending their whole life trying to find some fancy method that will get them into a trade at just the right point. Do you think that's a waste of time?

Not if you're a short-term trader. It's a requirement if you're an in-and-out trader or trying to buy bottoms and tops. I'm more of a commodity investor. That's a term you hardly ever see. I haven't used it in 10 years myself. When you look at my approach, it really is investing rather than trading.

INTERMEDIATE-TERM TRADERS

Kelly Angle

Kelly Angle, who recently stopped publishing his newsletter to become a full-time money manager, is an intermediate-term trader.

How do you rate the concept of trading with the trend?

When you say trend, I assume you mean major trend. Statistically, I've found over the long haul that taking positions in the direction of the major trend is better than trading against the trend. The problem with this conventional wisdom is that traders fall prey to the realization that once they put their trade on, the big move they hoped for often does not materialize. If the trade produces a profit of only $1,000, let's say, some traders are reluctant to take that size profit because the conception of trading with the major trend is to be able to capture major profits. Unfortunately, in today's environment most major trend trades do not produce major size profits.

If you're not going to trade with the major trend, what's the alternative? What do you do instead?

Statistically, you should trade with the major trend, period. The percentage accuracy and the amplitude of the move will be more favorable than trading against the trend.

Kelly Angle

K. D. (Kelly) Angle, age 42, is originally from Kansas and was introduced to the futures markets in 1979 while being groomed to assume operational control of his father's oil and gas exploration business. He witnessed his father make more than one hundred million dollars in realized and unrealized profits in a single gold position. Kelly has authored a book on his unique introduction to the markets: *One Hundred Million Dollars in Profits: An Anatomy of a Market Killing,* published by Windsor Books.

Kelly went on to develop his own trading strategies that evolved into an advisory service known as *The Timing Device* and a management company called K. D. Angle & Company. Both have been in business since 1986. Kelly claims to have a trading program with less inherent risk and with a smaller degree of potential volatility than others. He calls it *Cornucopia*. Since this interview, Kelly has become a full-time money manager.

Angle is currently working on a second book for John Wiley and Sons that will include many of the unconventional ideas that have contributed to his trading success. Angle resides and operates his company at 24 East Avenue, Box 1290, New Canaan, CT 06840. Phone (203) 972-1776. Fax (203) 972-3192.

In your time frame you should trade with the major trend. Whether you're trading for an hour or for a month, trade with the major trend. The amplitude and moves are going to be higher statistically and quantifiably than trading against the trend. There are guys out there though who love to trade against the trend.

If you want to trade shorter term, that's okay, but make sure that when you trade with the intermediate trend you're also trading with the longer-term trend?

Yes. Let's say you trade in a market that has been predominantly up over the last year. If you look at the breakdown of your short- and long-term trades, usually it's very one-sided. That's a function of the trend. For example, look at a market like T-bonds over the last two years (1992–93). All your money is going to be made on the long side of the market. I don't care how you're trading or what kind of strategy you're using. Your short trades were where your liability was. That's where you lost your money. That's one example, but you could test 50 different systems on that bond market and if the move was predominantly up, then your liability came from trying to countertrend trade.

What is your definition of a major trend?

You can define it by a moving average of anywhere from 40 days on out. I like in the neighborhood between a 50- and 60-day moving average for trend determination. Once you go out beyond 40, you're talking about a pretty slow-moving average.

When you use a moving average, do you look at whether the price is above or below it or do you look at the direction of the average?

I look at whether price is above or below the moving average.

Do you use different lengths for different markets, or do you use the same one?

I like to use the same moving average for all markets. I don't like to tailor my parameters. I use the same system parameters for every market.

Because?

I don't want to optimize any market. One thing I've found is even though a particular market may be quiet now, within the next three years it will probably become very active. So why try to optimize and tailor-make your system parameters for the current market environment?

I'm trying to trade the more active markets. Those markets have a similar look compared to the inactive markets. I want everything to be open and general to all the markets I'm trying to trade so I don't lock out potential future performance.

If a market is trending up for the purposes of your long-term indicator, is that all you need for an entry or do you use other methods to fine-tune your entries?

The methodology would be considered a breakout-type. I want to rest a market entry order above or below the current market action. I find that all indicators, whether you're looking at Stochastics, Directional Movement, Rate of Change, all those things respond after the market responds.

I did some research using traditional indicators that produced a determination of whether the major trend or the minor trend was up or down. When all the indicators were up, we would buy. I constructed daily charts with hourly bars to attempt to get a head start on the moves. If the market had moved enough to flip the indicators, instead of finding that out at the end of the day, which would not allow an entry until the next morning, we could see the signal developing at 10 or 11 o'clock in the morning.

Then you would enter?

I would enter intraday.

Would you do anything if by the end of the day the indicators had flipped back the other way, or would you just ignore that?

No, because all the indicators would have to be up or down for it to be a bona fide signal. That filters out the noise. I had two tiers of indicators in two different time frames, short and long term. When both time frames were up, I bought. Generally, when one was conflicting with the other, I'd go to the sidelines. The only time that occurs is after you've had an extended move. You have survived in a trade for maybe four weeks, and you have $9,000 in open profits. Now prices start to consolidate and create a shelf. Then the short-term action turns down. Instead of being stopped out by a retracement mechanism, the short-term indicator flips down and you exit. It's the best way to take out more than 65 to 90 percent of an extended move. But that kind of move doesn't happen very often.

By themselves, intraday indicators like Stochastics are pretty miserable, especially when you follow them intraday. I found that if you had a big move intraday that got you into the market, maybe the move for the next day or two would already be over. Now you have a big exposure problem. It doesn't matter if it happens during the day or at the end of the day.

I tried to enter intraday to cut the risk down, and it did to some degree. But then I realized that the nature of those kinds of indicators is such that they lag the market. It doesn't matter if they lag by an hour or a day, they lag the market.

They're late. They're out of control. They force you to get into the market when it's already moved three grand. Using that type of trend-following approach, you had to use market-generated stops. Maybe in a couple of days you might be able to move up some sort of Fibonacci-ratio stop or something like that. Market-generated stops generally run between $1,000 and $3,000 in active markets. That's too big a price tag.

I don't use that approach anymore. I used it very successfully for a year and a half. It was profitable 19 out of 21 years on a hypothetical test basis. I eventually decided I didn't want to use such big initial stops.

Now I have a system in which, when market prices have compressed, I can anticipate a breakout and then buy or sell on the breakout.

You use the long-term indicator as a setup, but you don't enter solely because it goes from short to long?

Right.

Peter Brandt

Also in the intermediate-term time frame is my old friend, Peter Brandt.

Peter, what do you think is the importance of trading with the trend?

Trading with the trend is a wonderful idea conceptually, but it's very difficult to implement in everyday practical terms. It's something to which people give lip service without necessarily understanding.

Trading with the trend is like saying you're in favor of motherhood and apple pie. The problem comes into play when you try to define trend. Like everything else in trading, trend is wonderfully identifiable in hindsight, but very difficult to grasp in real time.

What complicates it further is that what may be an uptrend to me may be a downtrend to another trader because no two traders are going to view the markets with the identical time frame orientation. A floor trader may define the trend as the last four ticks. A long-term position trader may not care about anything other than a monthly chart or a 40-day moving average. Many

Peter Brandt

Peter Brandt has been involved in the futures business since 1976. He is a graduate of the University of Minnesota and the founder and chief executive officer of Factor Research and Trading Co., Inc. The firm has three primary operating subsidiaries: Factor Trading Co., Inc.; Factor Publishing Company; and Covenant Investment Corporation.

Factor Trading Co., Inc., invests in foreign exchange markets, U.S. and international government debt securities, U.S. and international stock index markets, precious metals, energy markets, traditional commodities, and other derivatives for its own account. Since 1981, Factor Trading Co., Inc., has achieved a compounded annual rate of return of over 90 percent in its proprietary trading.

Factor Publishing Company provides research and price forecasting through *The Factor* newsletter service. *The Factor* newsletter is published monthly with an intraweek telephone hotline service. It has been one of the most consistently profitable newsletter services with drawdowns also consistently among the lowest in the industry. Peter likes to point out that *The Factor* has never had an unprofitable year.

Covenant Investment Corporation is an offshore investment company domiciled in the Bahamas. Its shares are available to non–U.S. citizens. Covenant invests in a variety of international futures markets.

Factor Research and Trading Co., Inc., is also engaged in a joint publishing project with John Magee, Inc., one of the oldest and most respected names in technical analysis. FRT and John Magee jointly produce *The John Magee Reporter,* a research newsletter aimed at identifying only the 10 biggest trends in the futures markets each year.

Write to Peter at JMR/Factor Publishing, P.O. Box 62100, Colorado Springs, CO 80962-2100. Phone (719)-471-6898.

people use the concept of trading with the trend to indicate there is only one trend at any given time in any given market.

While I agree with the concept of trading with the trend, I condition that agreement with two caveats. First, a trader must have a precise way to determine and define trend for himself. Second, he must realize that his trend may be different from somebody else's trend.

I use a combination of moving averages to define trend for me. I use 13-period moving averages on daily, weekly, and monthly prices. They give me a good fix for which way the trend is. I'm hesitant to take a trade that is opposite my defined trend.

Another important point is that the time frame of one's trading maneuvers has to be related to the time frame of one's trend definition. In other words, it makes no sense to identify trend on monthly or weekly charts and then be a day trader. If I'm a position trader and trading off weekly or monthly charts, I should not be concerned with trend on a day-to-day basis.

You indicated you measure trend using 13-bar moving averages on daily, weekly, and monthly charts. Do you require all three to be in the same direction before you take a trade?

I require the daily plus at least one of the other two to be in the same direction.

How do you use the moving average?

I look at the direction of the moving average lines to indicate the trend. I may at times use the moving average, particularly the daily, as an indication of support or resistance.

It doesn't matter where the price is in relation to the moving average line?

I evaluate that subjectively. If I see a market on a daily chart that is clearly in a congestion area, I'm not going to pay absolute attention to the direction of the moving average line. I'll use it in combination with other chart data.

Once the trend sets up in a particular direction, then you use classical chart patterns as your entry trigger?

That's correct.

Colin Alexander

Another intermediate-term trader is Colin Alexander.

Colin, is the trend really your friend?

Everybody will tell you that the trend is your friend, but unless you have a working definition of what a trend is, you have a real problem with putting the idea into practical effect. For example, one person's retracement within a trend is another person's change of trend. The practicality of using this concept requires that you have criteria for determining what a trend is for the purposes of trading.

My first and most important criterion is to look for a conspicuous pattern of consecutive higher highs and higher lows (uptrend) or lower highs and lower lows (downtrend) on a weekly chart. I also use trendlines on weekly charts to figure the appropriate trend direction.

How do you draw the trendlines?

Off highs and lows as I can find them. When you have three points of contact, then you have a fairly high probability that you have a trend.

The disadvantage of this approach is that it can be fantastic in financial markets, but in markets such as live hogs, which flop around all over the place, it can be very difficult to draw trendlines that mean anything because of enormous disparities at contract changeover. Nevertheless, what the nearest future is doing can give you a bit of a handle on the very big picture.

Take a market like live hogs. Because it's so difficult to get longer-term trends, does that mean you don't trade it at all or do you trade it differently?

I look for other signals and trade it differently.

Colin Alexander

Colin Alexander, Marquis of La Cerda, is an independent trader, businessman, author, and publisher of *The Wellspring Futures Newsletter* and the daily Wellspring telephone hotline service.

Colin is the author of *Capturing Full-Trend Profits in the Commodity Futures Markets*, published by Windsor Books and now into its third printing. He has recently completed a second book for Windsor called *Five Star Futures Trades*. It comprises a completely calibrated and easy-to-use system for identifying and trading the biggest moves, like the big sale of the British pound by George Soros in 1972.

Educated at Stowe (the famous English public school attended by people like David Niven and Prince Rainier of Monaco), Magdalen College, Oxford, and The Free University in West Berlin, Colin migrated to Canada in 1963. He has been a successful fur trader in the Arctic and a journalist, as well as a publisher and author.

In addition to the books discussed above, Colin has authored the widely acclaimed book, *The Ghost of the Yellowknife Inn*, a book of popular and humorous verse in the traditional style that might have come from the pen of Robert Frost, Ogden Nash, or Tom Lehrer. There are plans for a new edition, including more pieces particularly appealing to the business and financial community, under the potential title *Wall Street Fizz*.

Colin is domiciled in Ogdensburg in upstate New York and spends his time between there; Ottawa, Canada; and London, England. Apart from conventional recreational pursuits like skiing and swimming, he works at his verse and improving trading techniques.

Write to Colin at 812 Proctor Avenue, Ogdensburg, NY 13669. Phone (613)-745-5593.

Do you have any other trend-finding indicators?

There's a third parameter that I look at to try and answer the question "What is a trend?" On the daily chart I look at two moving averages, a 25-day and a 40-day. Conventional wisdom is that one looks to trade in the direction of a price crossover. I disregard that entirely. Moving averages for me acquire usefulness when they are showing a direction. There is an assumed uptrend if a moving average is pointing upward and there is an assumed downtrend if it is pointing down.

Sometimes there can be extra prime entry signals—for instance, when price crosses a moving average on the daily chart simultaneously with a direction change in the moving average, all within a day or two. You ideally prefer to have the confirmation of a strong close on the side of the moving average in the direction you are planning to trade.

Do you ever make trades against your trend indicators?

Occasionally there will be situations where there's an island left behind such as occurred in the precious metals markets last August. Occasionally I might take what would be construed as a contratrend trade if we're at very prominent support or resistance levels.

An example of a such a trade that unfortunately I did not take was the famous time when George Soros shorted the British pound at the $2.00 level in September 1992. It was very clear on the weekly and monthly charts that this was an extremely high point beyond which it was unlikely to proceed much further and from which some worthwhile decline might follow. You have to trade these things lightly, hold your breath and hope that they work.

Michael Chisholm

Another intermediate-term trader is Michael Chisholm.

How important a principle is trading with the trend?

From my perspective, it's almost so obvious it goes without saying. I can't imagine anyone trading against the trend and being consistently profitable.

To me the key is to determine first what length trend or cycle you're going

Michael Chisholm

As an analyst and student of market action for nearly three decades, Michael Chisholm brings the qualities of his genius, having an IQ that has been measured at 188, and the insight he has gained from his training as a therapist.

He has constantly published his newsletter, *Taurus*, since 1976. It was voted Number 1 in a poll of its readers by *Futures* magazine. Chisholm claims his published recommendations have netted over $1,250,000 trading single contracts over the past 10 years.

He has written 18 books and system manuals including *Games Investors Play* (1981) and *The Taurus Method* (1983). Additionally, he has created a number of audio and video instructional cassettes. He is listed in *Who's Who in the South*. Mr. Chisholm regularly appears on financial television programs.

He occasionally presents workshops and appears at seminars worldwide. Write to him at Taurus, P.O. Box 767, Winchester, VA 22604. Phone (703)-667-4827.

to trade. If you're trading short or very short-term, you're looking at a different kind of trend than if you're trading long-term or intermediate-term. Whether you're short-term trading or very short-term trading, the best way is to trade the shorter cycles when they're in agreement with the longer cycles. This cuts down on the trades, but it lines up all the different cycles so you're getting the real thrust, the real momentum of the trend.

There are a number of ways to do this. One of my most favorite ways is to use the 14-bar weekly Stochastics and/or monthly Stochastics or sometimes both in conjunction. When you have the weekly Stochastics or the monthly Stochastics heading in the direction of your trades, that is a powerful trend indicator.

You don't care what level it's at, you just want it moving up for longs and moving down for shorts?

I do look at the level. If we're at extraordinarily high Stochastics readings, I'll be loathe to pyramid as heavily as I might otherwise. I've seen Stochastics go up to where it is almost off the screen and stay there for weeks on end while the move continues up. I'm not a believer that once Stochastics pass a certain level, it's time to get out because I've seen too many occasions where that doesn't hold up.

From a psychological standpoint, I've encountered a number of friends, clients, and subscribers over the years who want to be different. They want to beat the market, and they insist on trading against the trend. They sometimes call themselves contrarians. Once in a great while they will hit a streak and turn out okay. They'll catch a bottom or catch a top. But overall that's a road to ruin. It's hard enough to beat the markets when you're trading with the trend, much less going against the trend. When a trader believes he has to show how smart he is by being able to beat the market against the trend, things are not going to turn out well.

When I devise a new system, the first thing I look for is what methodology am I going to use to determine how the market is trending.

You indicated the time period you're going to trade is important. What time period do you prefer?

The methodology I have that works best of all encompasses trades that run between 30 and 60 days. I call them short-term trades, but they're really intermediate-term trades. With them I most definitely try to have the weekly Stochastics in my favor and generally the monthly Stochastics as well.

If you're trading a 30- to 60-day time frame, you're looking at daily charts?

Yes.

What kind of trend indicator do you use on daily charts?

I have a number of them that I look at. I use different bar lengths of Wilder's Directional Movement Index. Different bar lengths of Momentum. I watch

ADX, the level of the ADX, and whether it's rising or falling.

How do you interpret ADX in terms of trend?

Despite what some of the articles and books I've read have said, I have found that the ADX typically rises in a rising market and falls in a falling market. I use a 14-bar ADX and look at its four-day Momentum. If the ADX today is lower than the ADX of four days ago and our other trend indicators confirm, that's an indication that the trend has changed and is heading down. I never rely upon just one trend indicator. I require several to agree.

Once you determine the trend from weekly, monthly, and daily charts, then do you have a trigger that gets you into a trade?

Right. What I'm doing by using daily, weekly, and monthly charts is getting the different length cycles into alignment. Although I'm not measuring the cycles *per se*, I'm using the Stochastics readings as a surrogate.

When all the indicators come into alignment, a typical entry trigger would be to put a resting buy or sell order between one and three ticks above or below the extreme of the market on the day everything comes into alignment. That is one final confirmation. Sometimes I'll have everything come into alignment, put a resting buy stop two ticks above the high of the day, and the next day the market crashes. It helps keep me out of those kinds of bad markets.

How do you follow these indicators? Do you use a computer program?

No, I use our CQG screens (Commodity Quotegraphics intraday quote system). Every afternoon my vice president, Ginny Carnell, and I sit down before the markets close at about 1 o'clock. We work at the screens until about 4:30 PM doing all of our analysis. It takes about three and a half hours. We come to the office early in the morning, too. I get there between 3 and 4 AM. Ginny comes in about 7 AM. We spend about an hour going over the charts again looking at anything that we questioned from the night before or anything we thought of overnight. In total we spend somewhere between four and a half to five hours a day at our screens.

Bill Gary

Another intermediate-term trader is fundamentalist, Bill Gary.

How important to successful trading is following the trend?

I learned a lesson about that last summer. There are two basic trends that I follow. The first is on the weekly charts. I put a great deal of long-term emphasis on the weekly trend. What I call the intermediate trend is looking at trendlines on a daily chart.

Last summer I was very bullish on the grains and was long going into the summer. I didn't pay any attention to breaking those intermediate-term trendlines in July because I knew the long-term trend was still up. I ended up riding those things all the way down into late summer while the long-term trend continued holding bullish. It turned out fine in the end, but I'd have been a lot better off if I had gotten out and then reentered after the break. Now I put more emphasis on the daily chart trends as a method of moving out of the way of setbacks or adverse moves.

In terms of being a successful trader overall, how important is the concept of trading with the trend?

It's imperative. I've never known anyone who traded in and out of the markets using oscillators or overbought/oversold indicators as their prime indicators, who has ever made any money and kept it. The people who make the big money catch the big moves. They don't trade in and out, and they don't trade against the trend.

Okay, if you're looking at daily charts now primarily instead of monthly or weekly, how many days does the market have to move in a particular direction before you're satisfied that's the trend? What kind of time frame are you looking at to establish a trend?

To end an uptrend I wait for an RSI sell signal from an overbought area and wait until the ADX line has turned down. These indicate that the intermediate trend has ended. Before exiting a long position I also like to see a top formation on the chart. The converse would work for a bear market. I give the market plenty of latitude and plenty of room.

Bill Gary

Bill Gary majored in financial management at Southern Illinois University. He began his commodity career as a corn buyer for a large milling firm in Central Illinois. Over a six-year period as corn buyer and director of hedging operations, he gained invaluable experience in both cash and futures markets. Bill began to trade futures for his own account in 1961 and has been an active trader since that time.

After gaining insight as a cash grain buyer and hedger, Bill joined an internationally respected research firm to gain knowledge and experience in market research and commodity price forecasting. During two years as feed grain researcher for Longstreet Abbott and Company in St. Louis, Bill designed hedging programs and prepared monthly price forecasts for some of America's largest milling and processing firms.

Bill became a partner in a small regional brokerage firm in 1967 as vice president and research director. In 1968, he established his own research firm, Commodity Information Systems (CIS), that publishes a newsletter and provides research services to leading agricultural industries. CIS gained an international reputation following its forecast for record high grain prices in 1972, six to nine months before the historic bull markets began.

Bill's newsletter, now named *Price Perceptions,* was the first major publication to explain deflationary market forces in 1980 and why they would end the commodity price spiral. He was the subject of a feature article in *Forbes* magazine for advising clients to short stock indices before the Crash of 1987.

He has been featured frequently in *Barrons, The Wall Street Journal, Pro Farmer, The Farm Journal,* and other leading national publications.

For a free sample of his newsletter write CIS / Price Perceptions 210 Park Avenue, Suite 2970, Oklahoma City, OK 73102. Phone (800)-231-0477 or (405)-235-5687. Fax (405)-232-4354.

How do you determine what the intermediate-term trend is from the daily chart? Is it whether RSI is above or below 50?

No. I use basic, long-term trendlines even on a daily chart.

If you use a break of the trendline to get to the sidelines, what would cause you to turn bearish and say the trend is down?

I go back to the weekly chart. If our weekly chart is still in an uptrend, I do not go short.

So you want the weekly trendline and the daily trendline to be in agreement before you'll initiate a position?

Right.

And it's exiting a position where you use the daily chart alone.

Yes.

SHORT-TERM TRADERS

Stan Tamulevich

In the short-term trader category, I found Stan Tamulevich.

Stan, what do you think of the concept of trading with the trend?

Trading with the trend is something we all think very highly of, and so do I. In preparing for this interview, I looked at my last 19 trades since the first of February. Incredibly, 58 percent were clearly countertrend trades. Incredibly as well, I made six times the profit in my countertrend trades versus my trend-following trades. It really floored me because I know the importance of thinking in terms of trend.

When I look at the trend, I look at the 10-week and the 20-day trends. I use them for reference. I get a feel for the market. I don't use them as a signal,

Stan Tamulevich

A science and biology graduate of both the Universities of Michigan and Wisconsin, Stan Tamulevich traded science for an investment career in 1969. He started as a broker for Bache & Co. His specialty has been short-term trading. A student of the go-go years of the late sixties and the bear markets that followed, Stan learned to concentrate on short-term trading and consequently fell in love with commodities.

Independent since 1980, Stan currently manages accounts, has a daily telephone/fax advisory called *Marketline Update,* and publishes trading techniques and systems. His materials are suited to both beginners and professionals.

Concentrating on discipline and money management has contributed to a successful 25 years in commodities. He points out that "The lessons learned since the seventies continue to bear fruit in the nineties. The script is not that much different. Only the players change. Human emotion and psychology remain a constant." Stan adds, "I recommend that traders borrow from the best ideas available and modify them to fit their style and comfort level."

He is always willing to share his accumulated experience. Feel free to call him at (608)-277-8734. Write for information to One Georgetown Court, Madison, WI 53719.

but as a reference point. You really have to be disciplined to do countertrend trades, and that's what my trading is all about, strict discipline.

The fact of the matter is trends do run, they do get extended, and it's a dangerous game trying to be a countertrend trader. But there is a point where you can recognize that a market is very ripe to change direction, and that's where I try to capitalize on it, mostly with stop entries.

I'm actually very uncomfortable with long-term trades.

Why?

The moves are so dramatic in terms of your equity. To take a position and have it move $600 or $800 in your favor and then to watch it give back maybe 80 percent of that is not my idea of comfort when you're trading.

So you gravitate toward a shorter time frame just because of the comfort level.

Exactly. I don't use any computerized technology. I read the charts one day at a time, and I update my charts manually. The charts really talk to me. I get a feel for when something is about to change, and when I ought to be looking for a trade. It jumps out at you. I can update my charts one day and draw a complete blank. I do them the next day, and there's a trade right there.

How long have you been doing that?

Since 1971.

How long do you think it would take somebody to get the kind of experience that you have that enables you to trade like that?

You could do it in two or three years if you had a real good feel for it. You would have to keep your charts manually for at least a couple of years.

So you don't really look at trend the way most people do. You don't have a requirement that the market be trending a certain way before you take a trade. You're more short term than that. You're just looking at a few days of market action. Would that be a fair statement?

Probably so. Momentum figures a lot into what I do. If, for example, you look at a low having been touched and then you get a small rally and a downward zigzag, an A-B-C mini-pattern, and the market doesn't fail again, that's an excellent opportunity for a long trade using a buy-stop entry. It's those types of things I look for.

You want the market moving in your direction even if only for a little bit.

Exactly. Often, however, if I'm especially comfortable with a trade, I will enter at the market on the opening.

James Kneafsey

Another short-term trader is James Kneafsey.

What is your opinion of the principle that you should trade with the trend?

In theory this is a very noble idea, but in practice it is fairly difficult. This is partially because the markets are not clearly trending all the time. In fact, from my research about a third of the time the markets are in what I call either a wide chop or a minor trend. Another third of the time there is a neutral or sideways move. Ideally it's something I support and try to do, but it's not easy. If I were ranking your four principles, this would not be at the top.

If you're not trading with the trend, what are you doing?

You're trying to be ready to go with the trend. In other words, you always want to make sure you don't miss the trend. You have to have a position one way or the other. You might use an options strategy to hedge your trend position. You can at least avoid any significant loss to offset a futures reversal or when there's no trend by compensating in an options trade.

In terms of trading with the trend, you need some definition of what a trend is for you, right?

Yes.

Can you give me one?

Indeed I can. Our trading system is always long or short if by our definition there is a trend. We have 16 technical variables and 1 fundamental variable. That fundamental variable is a six-month fundamental forecast, which is a minor component in the whole list of items. Among the 16 technical variables are 3 trend variables. One is a Stochastic measure. Another is Welles Wilder's Directional Movement, which has to be positive. The third is a moving average combination that has to be positive. When all three are positive, we have an uptrend. When all three are negative, we have a downtrend. That is an unequivocal measurement—when those three technical variables are all in the same configuration.

James Kneafsey

James T. Kneafsey, Ph.D., is a founder and president of both Cambridge Financial Management, Inc. (established in 1987) and Cambridge Commodities Corporation (established in 1977). In these capacities, he has developed a wide range of forecasting models in equity, fixed-income, commodity, and foreign exchange rate markets. These models form the foundation for each firm's trading programs for institutional, plan sponsor, and corporate clients.

Prior to starting his own firms, Dr. Kneafsey was a full-time faculty member in M.I.T.'s Civil Engineering Department. He also has taught or lectured at the University of Pittsburgh, Princeton, Harvard, and the University of North Carolina.

He is the author of two books and several scholarly articles on applied economics and industrial organization and has served on retainer to numerous corporations, financial firms, and government agencies. He has a Ph.D. in Economics from Ohio State University (1971), an M.A. from the University of Florida, and a B.A. in English and Mathematics from Loyola College. He is currently a visiting professor at M.I.T., teaching a course on global financial markets at the Center for Advanced Engineering Studies.

Dr. Kneafsey has traded in the futures and options markets for 18 years. Dr. Kneafsey's work to date has resulted in proprietary price forecasting models for several products unique to the industry and the development of the Cambridge Currency Overlay Programs, which are considered to be in the vanguard of investment management.

Write to Jim at Cambridge Financial Management, Inc., 55 Cambridge Parkway, Riverfront 2, Cambridge, MA 02142. Phone (617)-621-8500.

Let's take one at a time. When you use Stochastics, do you use the same time length for all markets?

No. We have done computer testing over the years and we assign each a slightly different length, but they tend to vary from 9 to 16 days.

So you have optimized your variables for the markets. What do you say to those many people who say that's very dangerous to do?

I've found it to be useful because we reoptimize every quarter. We keep it up as a piece of research, and it can be very expensive to do that. But I don't rely strictly on Stochastics. I look for Stochastics to call a turning point in the trend.

Normally the way people use Stochastics as a trend indicator is when it's over 50 or under 50. Do you use it that way?

Yes. We also look at the extreme points where we use 75 and 30 as the extreme thresholds. It carries a dual function. One is to signify when a trend is beginning, and the second is to indicate when a trend may be close to completion. The Stochastic influences the trailing stop on a position. When it reaches overbought, that would influence the trailing sell stop (on a long position) to move faster than it would otherwise.

Another indicator you listed was Directional Movement. Do you use different lengths of Directional Movement for different markets as well?

Yes. There's less variability there—10 to 14.

Then there was a two-moving average setup?

Yes. The short-term must be above the long-term and both must be moving up for a positive trend. The short-term must be below the long-term and both must be moving down for a downtrend. Those are our three primary trend indicators.

Is that an absolute filter so that you won't take a long position unless all three of those are positive?

No. Nothing is absolute in trading. One of the 16 is our famous Cambridge Hook, and that can override everything else. There's a certain amount of discretion. But on balance I would say four out of five trades have to be consistent with that pattern where all three are positive or all three are negative. The odds are that once all three turn positive or negative, they remain that way for multiple days.

Judging by the length of your indicators, they are fairly short-term. So you're trying to get into trends fairly early?

Yes. That ties in with your second principle of cutting losses short.

Glen Ring

Another short-term trader is Glen Ring.

Glen, how important is trading with the trend to you?

While trading with the trend is very important, it's not *the* key. It is one of the pieces of the puzzle. It's vital to adapt your trading style to your own personality.

With that said, for the vast majority, trading with the trend is very important. If you haven't become an expert at the trading process, the most forgiving way to trade is with the trend.

The first thing you have to do before you can trade with the trend is take some time to define what a trend is to you. There are numerous people out there who say they want to trade with the trend, but when you ask them to define a trend, they can't. There are an infinite number of ways to identify trends, but the key is to have some specific methodology. It's important to develop a strategy that will allow you to identify a trend at its earliest possible moment.

Are there guidelines you can give people about the choices they might make when they are trying to decide what trend means to them?

You want to focus on learning how to trade. Try to master simple techniques first. In the beginning, define a simple way to identify trends and master that. Either use a moving average or the principle of higher highs and

Glen Ring

Glen Ring has over 20 years of market experience. His market activity started as an agricultural producer. From this, he followed his love of markets into positions as a broker, an analyst, a consultant to floor traders, manager of a marketing firm, and a trader.

Glen is the editor of *Trends in Futures,* a weekly newsletter available via mail or fax providing analysis on 34 markets. The newsletter is primarily based on technical and psychological analysis, with tips for traders and other market participants. Glen also produces *Trader Update,* a daily fax and electronic update on current markets. He has also contributed numerous articles to *Futures* magazine and created a videotape lecture series.

Glen is a popular seminar leader and conference speaker — who gets high praise for his ability to communicate a common sense approach to futures trading and analysis.

While continuing his high-quality analysis, Glen has focused much of his work in the 1990s on the process of trading— compiling what it takes to be a consistently successful trader.

Write to Glen at Futures, P.O. Box 6, Cedar Falls, IA 50613. Phone (800)-221-4352 or (319)-277-1276.

higher lows to mark uptrends and lower highs and lower lows to mark downtrends. If you're going to use higher highs and lower lows, be sure to define precisely what qualifies as a high and a low.

Isn't the time frame important, too?

It can be. For me, a time frame is important in developing a swing pattern for trends. But time is not necessarily crucial because if it were, point and figure charts wouldn't work. Point and figure charts eliminate time.

It comes down to having definitions. Define as much as you possibly can so you leave as little as possible to guesswork.

How do you define trend?

For long positions, I look for swing patterns of higher highs and higher lows. The minimum reaction to make a swing is three days.

Are you using daily or weekly charts?

I use both. I identify different degrees of trend. I determine the trend on a daily, weekly, and even monthly degree.

TREND CHANGE ANTICIPATORS
Phyllis Kahn

I spoke to several advisors/traders who attempt to anticipate changes in trend rather than wait for them to occur. One was Phyllis Kahn.

Phyllis, how important is trading with the trend to a Gann disciple?

I think trading with the trend is very important. You have to know what the trend is, and in my work the only way you can know that is by looking at monthly and weekly charts. Before we begin to trade with the trend, we must understand what time period we are trading in. I'm a position trader. Someone who is day trading doesn't have to know the trend of more than an hourly chart because to them an hourly chart would be the equivalent of a monthly chart to me. It's still important to trade with the trend even if you're an in-and-out day trader.

Assuming you know what your trading time frame is, how do you determine the trend?

In order to enter or exit a market, signals have to be in place on a weekly basis. I use certain indicators, time periods, multiples of time periods, and

Phyllis Kahn

Phyllis Kahn writes the only "pure Gann" newsletter. Called *Gann Angles*, she has been publishing it monthly since 1983. Kahn is no stranger to experienced traders as she has been speaking and giving Gann seminars for 15 years.

After two years of college, she was sidetracked by an early marriage. She dropped her economics studies to put her husband through medical school. Three children and 19 years later, she was finally ready to begin her own career.

She and a woman friend had a gambling kitty to play with every year on winter vacations. In 1969, they decided to take their current stake of a few thousand dollars to a commodity brokerage house instead. "We knew nothing and so decided to sit quietly and watch what went on," she explained. "We listened to the brokers trade pork bellies. After a few weeks, we decided that the best way to succeed was to fade the brokers."

As you might expect from her strategy of going contrary to the brokers, Phyllis was an instant success. She began to trade for relatives, and the next logical step was to become a broker herself.

In 1976, Kahn discovered W. D. Gann. "This was what I had been looking for. I began to spend my evenings creating weekly and monthly Gann-style charts in all the important commodities. It took me two years of constant effort. I gave up my social life and worked literally seven days a week. I have been committed to the Gann methods ever since."

For aspiring Gannians, Phyllis recommends Gann's book, *How to Make Profits in Commodities*. "Any time someone wants to sell you anything over four digits that's supposed to contain Gann secrets, run, do not walk, to the nearest exit," she warns.

Phyllis currently lives in Carmel, California. She manages accounts for others, trades her own account, and publishes the newsletter. Write to Phyllis at 495 Trinity Avenue, Suite A, Seaside, CA 93955, or call (408)-393-2000.

clusters of time to enter. When I take a trade from a weekly chart, I expect it to be a multiweek trade. If it doesn't go my way right away, then I'm out. It has to go my way.

What kind of indicators do you look at?

The most important are my Gann timer indicators, which are 100 percent related to time. I have a certain week and a certain day within the week where I'm expecting a reversal. I wait for the reversal to occur before entering. I place a buy stop or a sell stop for entry, and I let the market put me in.

I take a position through entering buy stops (for reversals to the upside) and sell stops (for reversals to the downside) a certain distance from the extreme low or high. I use a different distance from the bottom (or top) for each market. I place these stop orders automatically when my clusters of time are due.

There is a short time window. It is only a couple of days on each side of the target day. If the market doesn't hit my entry stops right away, I cancel them.

How long is the time window?

Five days.

How far does the market have to move from the extreme to get you in?

In the S&P, for long positions it is 40 points above the previous day's high in the time window. For short positions it is 40 points below the previous day's low in the time window.

Conceivably, you could be in the day after the low.

I could be in the day of the low.

What cycle lengths do you use to generate your time clusters?

The shortest cycle I use to generate these time clusters is three months, a 90-calendar-day cycle. I also use 90 trading days, 120 calendar and trading days, 144 calendar and trading days, and 180 calendar and trading days. I use all those cycles, so when I get a signal it is a really good signal. I'm not picking a bottom or a top. I'm requiring the market to reverse before I enter.

How did you get 40 points? Where did that come from?

It was just observational.

For different markets the length is different, but you use the same principle in all markets?

Yes. The cluster of time cycles is the initiating factor.

If you can actually get in on the bottom day, how can you say this is not bottom picking?

Because the market has to reverse from a down market to an up market.

It would be easy for someone to take the same general approach and modify it slightly by requiring a little more confirmation. For instance, they could require a day with a higher low and then after that put in the order 40 points above the high.

Right.

In all fairness, Phyllis, you're not really trading with the trend. You're trading against the trend. You're trading in anticipation that the trend will change. But the advantage it gives you is a low risk if you are wrong.

Exactly. If you're using an entry buy stop, you're going to place your protective sell stop just below the low that was created. So it gives you very low-risk trades.

If by trading with the trend someone means trading with an established trend, then you don't think that's important?

I don't think it's important for my trading system, no. In fact, I'm doing just the reverse. In that sense mine is not trading with the trend. It's trading against the trend. Only you're not stepping up unless you get a reversal.

A small reversal.

Once a new trend has been established, of course, you can stay in these trades for quite a while by just moving a trailing stop behind the position. Over time, you manage to catch some major reversal points.

Tom Aspray

Another trader who tries to anticipate changes in trend is Tom Aspray.

Tom, trading with the trend is not that important a principle to you, is it?

No, but it's where most of the money is made. Most of the time the market is not trending. During that roughly 70 percent of the time, I use one set of guidelines. During the 30 percent of the time when the market is trending, I use different strategies. Looking at a long-term profit/loss analysis, certainly the bulk of the profits will come from the trending periods. It's important to me in that it brings in a whole new set of trading rules that I use in that kind of market.

This is a kind of asset allocation. I take an initial position and as evidence emerges that the market is trending, I use any reactions to add contracts until I establish a full position. For example, if I have a maximum size of 10 contracts, I only reach that point in a trending market. If I can catch one or two big trending moves a year, that's great.

Let's talk about your first position. You're willing to take your first position before a trend is clearly established.

Yes.

It's the later contracts that you put on in the big moves.

My determination that it's a trending market changes my risk management style considerably and allows me to stay with the position much longer.

Tom Aspray

Thomas E. Aspray is recognized internationally as a pioneer in computerized technical market analysis. Since 1982, he has delivered foreign exchange market analysis to the institutional investment community, and his methods are now used by many other professional analysts. He has also conducted training programs for foreign exchange managers and dealers in Europe, Asia, and the United States.

Aspray's daily fax analysis service, *Aspray's Forex Trader*, is distributed to currency market professionals in the world's major countries and is respected worldwide for its unhedged views on the dollar. His analysis covers not only key trading levels for all major spots and crosses, but also the big picture in the world's financial markets and the impact of international events on currency valuations.

In addition to daily reports with short-term trading recommendations, Tom also develops intermediate-term currency trend analysis using his proprietary methods. His commentary includes both reviews of activity and what to look for in the coming trading week. He also publishes special reports following the release of important economic data or in response to changes in the market.

Aspray has been quoted extensively in the financial media, including *The Wall Street Journal, CNBC,* and *Futures* magazine. He is also the co-author of *The Business One Guide to the Futures Markets,* one of the country's leading books on technical analysis. He has been a speaker at many CompuTrac seminars worldwide.

Write to Tom Aspray at P.O. Box 2141, Spokane, WA 99210-2141. Phone (509)-838-0434.

Would it be a fair statement that in your initial trading you're anticipating a change in trend?

Yes.

How long after an extreme, a top or a bottom, are you willing to make an entry? How close to the top or bottom are you willing to start your initial position?

Quite close. I use a series of technical studies, and based on the strength of those signals I'll often start a position fairly close to what turns out to be the important high or low. If you're looking at something like the Herrick Payoff Index or On Balance Volume, which has multiple, positive divergences, you could also be seeing similar formations on the daily and weekly charts. You take a position when those divergences are confirmed and add to that position later when the market moves into a trending mode.

How close in days to the bottom could you conceivably get in?

Often times I'm even a day or two early before the bottom. If I'm stopped out on that first position, I usually have the presence of mind to get back in. I would say two or three days on either side.

Can you tell us what the difference is between the methods you use when the trend is not clearly established and when it is?

If I see no signs of trending, I will tend to accept small profits. I take a position for three to five days and use fairly tight stops. I'm not willing to risk much on those trades. If we're in a trending market, I'll use a wider stop and give the trade more room. I then tend to scale out of my position once I see some signs we're moving from a trending to a nontrending mode again.

Do you have a way to define that a trend is clearly established?

I use a combination of the ADX and the ADXR from Wilder's Directional Movement Index. I've combined several other methods along with ADX and ADXR into something I call the APM Trend Watch. It is an indicator that goes from zero to plus four, and I run a moving average of it as well.

Historically, if it moves above the plus two level, that's the trending mode. In a strongly trending market it will stay locked at plus four. The ADX as a proxy will continue to rise maybe up towards 50 or 60. Then as the APM Trend Watch starts to turn down, that is the initial sign the trend is weakening.

What exactly is the APM Trend Watch?

It is proprietary, but it looks at the relationship between the ADX and the ADXR, whether ADX is above ADXR. I use a 9-period as opposed to a 14-period ADX. There are some other ingredients in there, some moving averages and some other sophisticated linear regression channeling methods that also give me an idea of a trending versus a nontrending market.

You have four indicators and when they're all positive, that's a plus four?

Exactly.

Do you run your indicators mostly on daily, weekly, or monthly charts?

For trading I use dailies. For picking an important bottom or top, the weekly is more important. I need to see some sign that there is a significant change from my weekly analysis before I start to take a trending position based on daily analysis. First weekly, then daily.

Robert Miner

Another Gann disciple and trend-change anticipator is Robert Miner.

How important do you think it is to trade with the trend?

It's critical. I don't know how you trade against the trend. The trend is relative to the time period that you're trading. You must have a methodology that would give you an understanding of what's the position of the market within whatever time frame it is you're looking to trade. As an example, I typically look to trade what I call intermediate-term, which is usually anywhere from about three weeks to three months. I'm looking at intermediate-term swings, those trends that are going to last several weeks.

How do you identify what the trend is in your time frame?

Robert Miner

Robert Miner is an active futures trader and the author of the *Dynamic Trader* software program. *Dynamic Trader* is a unique technical analysis program. It includes a comprehensive training course on the techniques incorporated in the program and teaches traders the trading strategies to integrate the analysis into a comprehensive, organized trading plan. Miner is also the editor and publisher of the monthly *Dynamic Trader Analysis Report* and weekly *Dynamic Trader Weekly Fax Report.*

Miner's monthly and weekly advisory reports focus on providing subscribers with a trading education. Each monthly report includes a comprehensive trading tutorial of practical analysis and trading strategy techniques or a comprehensive market research report. Each weekly fax report also includes a thorough explanation of the analysis used in the trading decisions. Miner believes that it is as important to educate traders to understand the analysis techniques and trading strategies as it is to provide market forecasts and trading recommendations.

He believes his most important contribution to the field of technical analysis has been his unique methods of time and price analysis and projection techniques and the ability to integrate these methods with practical trading strategies.

Miner was the 1993 first place winner of the Robbins Trading Company World Cup Championship of Futures Trading, Professional Division. This was a real time, real money, year-long trading contest.

He has contributed articles to *Futures* magazine, *Technical Analysis of Stocks and Commodities*, *Gann/Elliott Technician*, *Trader's World Magazine,* and *Geometric Research Forum.*

Write to Robert Miner at Dynamic Traders Group, Inc., 6336 N. Oracle, Suite 326-346, Tucson, AZ 85704. Phone (520)-797-3668. Fax (520)-797-2045.

I don't have an objective way of saying this is the trend. I do all my work with time and price. A certain time and price relationship tells me a trend change has occurred. How important the trend change will be is relative to the degree of swing on which I've done my projections. If I've calculated my projections from intermediate-term swings and then there is a time/price setup, then more than likely it's going to be an intermediate-term trend change. In addition, I use Elliott Wave patterns to describe which degree of trend I'm in.

You're not looking so much for a trend to be established. You're looking for a place to identify a change in trend fairly quickly.

Absolutely. From my point of view, by the time the trend is established and recognized as a particular degree of trend, it's almost over. At least we're so far into it that it becomes very difficult to enter the market.

So you don't use trend indicators like most other people do. Most people say the trend is important. I want to trade with a particular intermediate-term trend and therefore until the trendline is up or the 23-day Momentum is up or a Moving Average or whatever, I don't take any long trades. You don't do anything like that.

Nothing like that. By the time that kind of signal comes, I have no more interest in trading the market because it's so far along, all the safe entry points are past.

You recognize that you want to trade with the trend, but you're always trying to anticipate the confirmation of a change in trend rather than waiting for it.

I'm looking to anticipate and recognize when the trend change occurs at the time that it occurs, and then identify a confirmation that the trend change has occurred.

What kind of a confirmation do you require?

One has to do with pattern: taking out a prior swing high or low. That's a simple one. A more delayed confirmation uses Elliott Wave Theory. It is a potential Wave Three that exceeds the length and percentage in price and time of Wave One. More than likely that would not be a countertrend, but rather a new impulse trend.

By the time you get to Wave Three isn't the move about over?

Yes, but I'm already in it. I've usually entered before the confirmation.

So you don't need any confirmation.

Not to enter, no.

But you do need some confirmation apparently. You have these projected dates on which you're looking for a change in trend, but you don't just enter on that date; you wait for something else to happen.

Right.

What is it that you wait for?

I wait for the market to go into a projected time period at the same time that it's trading into a projected price period. Those time and price projections are ones that typically result in a trend change. Let's say I'm looking at intermediate-degree swings and doing projections from them. If a market moves into a time projection at the same time it moves into a price projection, then the probabilities are the market will change trend at that point. The third confirmation is the pattern. The pattern is what I call a termination pattern, meaning one that says, "This particular degree of trend is finished."

Can you give me an example of what a termination pattern looks like?

A fifth wave of a fifth wave. Most of the pattern analysis is based on Elliott Wave.

Will you enter a market while it's moving against the direction you want to trade in, or do you require price to be moving in your favor?

Do I pick tops and bottoms?

Do you?

Yes. Most of my trades are entered when I believe it's a top or a bottom.

You're buying weakness and selling strength at these turning points.

Yes.

You're always trying to trade with the trend. It's just that you don't use trend identification the same way other people do.

Exactly.

UNIQUE TREND-FINDING MECHANISMS
Walter Bressert

Some traders have a totally unique way to consider trend. Walter Bressert's market analysis always proceeds from cycle analysis. He was one of the original cycle gurus in the early 1970s.

Walt, how does the trend fit in with cycle analysis?

Trading with the trend is one of the most important things you can do. When I first started trading 25 years ago, an old trader gave me some advice. I remember his words exactly: "Kid, trading the market is easy. You trade with the trend. You buy the dips and sell the rallies." I figured he handed me the Holy Grail. The questions remain How do you define the trend? and How do you identify the dips and the rallies?

The trend is your friend. If something is going to happen adversely or if there's a surprise news story that has an impact, it's much more likely to occur in the direction of the trend. Markets tend to move more easily in the direction of the trend. When they correct against the trend, they're slower.

So as a trader, I do want to trade with the trend. I want to buy dips because

Walter Bressert

Walter Bressert is acknowledged as the man who brought cycle analysis to the futures markets in his original newsletter *HAL Commodity Cycles*, published between 1974 and 1985. It was profitable 10 of 12 years, and rated number 1 in bull markets by *Futures* magazine.

Walter retired in 1985, and in 1991 published his book, *The Power of Oscillator/Cycle Combinations.* Currently, he publishes the *CycleWatch* newsletter, which forecasts time and price moves weeks and months into the future. *CycleWatch* is available as both a newsletter and daily fax-on-demand, and via DBC Signal, FutureLink, and DTN. Walter's trading recommendations are also featured on the AllStar Advisors Hotline — 1/900-288-2262, extension 4. He teaches how to trade with cycles and oscillators in his at-home study course. Most recently Walter has developed *CycleFinder*, a powerful software program that finds cycles in any market, in any time frame.

He was one of the original founders of CompuTrac before it was purchased by Telerate/Dow Jones, and is a long-standing director of the nonprofit Foundation for the Study of Cycles. He has lectured internationally for 20 years and written articles for *The Wall Street Journal, Barrons, Futures* magazine, and the *Commodity Research Bureau Yearbook.* He was a contributing editor to the Financial News Network.

Write to Walter at P.O. Box 8268, Vero Beach, FL 32963. Phone (407)-388-3330.

I can get a good position in the direction of the trend with low dollar risk.

How do you determine what trend length you will trade?

I trade in the direction of the next longer cycle to the one I'm actually trading. Every market has dominant cycles. The three most important to me are the seasonal cycle, the weekly (or primary) cycle, and the daily (or trading) cycle.

I call the weekly cycle the primary cycle because it's of primary importance to trade with the trend and that's the trend I use. The trading cycle is an approximate four-week cycle that I use to trade the markets.

Once I identify a primary cycle bottom of an established length, I've got an idea of trend. I've got the trend until that cycle tops. By studying the past, I can anticipate approximately the price range and time frame of that cycle to make a top. That means the trend will end at least for a period of time, and it may even reverse. The same holds true for identifying a cycle top.

If you trade with what you call the trading cycle, then it's the weekly cycle that you use to establish the overall trend.

The weekly cycle establishes the trend. I'm searching for the bottom of the weekly cycle. As the market is going down, I have a time and price objective for the bottom. I'm looking at oscillators, market geometry, and everything I can find to help me identify when this cycle is going to bottom because that's going to be a trend reversal. I want not only to trade with the trend, but I want to catch trend reversals.

Let's say the seasonal cycle is currently moving up and the primary cycle is moving down. I know that soon we're going to have a bottom of the primary cycle. I want to look for a way to buy the bottom of that primary cycle. The bottom of that primary cycle is also going to be the bottom of a trading cycle. I'm going to combine the two cycles to try to find that bottom.

When I say I try to buy the bottom, I don't mean the low tick or the low day. There's only one low tick, and there's only one low day. If you fish for those, you often fish several times before you find the right one. By buying the bottom, I mean letting the market make its bottom and then give technical indications the bottom is in place, either on a daily or intraday basis.

You want to buy those indicators at the bottom of a primary cycle and a trading cycle with the expectation that a good uptrend is beginning. After the bottom occurs and as the uptrend continues, you look to buy the dips. The dips are the trading cycle and half-cycle lows. Every trading cycle has a half-trading cycle. Since the normal trading cycle is four weeks, you've got a half-cycle of about two weeks. You're looking for a dip about every two weeks and every other one of those is a sizable dip, a good buying dip.

What kind of confirmation of the bottom do you look for?

Confirmation comes from different time frames. Your most solid confirmation is going to come from a weekly or monthly perspective. I evaluate the market on monthly, half-monthly, weekly, daily, half-daily, hourly, 13-minute, 5-minute and 7-minute time segments. Looking to confirm a bottom of the weekly cycle, the most solid confirmation is generally going to come using the weekly or the half-monthly time period. By the nature of those time periods, they're big. That means when you get the confirmation, you're quite a ways away from the bottom and your dollar risk is big.

I use that for my final confirmation, but as a trader I try to get in closer to the bottom, which means entering before I have a confirmation. I do that with the trading cycle. If I can identify the bottom of the trading cycle within hours, days, or a week at the most, then I can get in near the bottom. If I indeed have the primary cycle bottom, that low should not be taken out until the cycle has topped. I'm talking about at least weeks and often months before a top. In trying to buy the bottom of a weekly cycle, I'm going to use daily and even hourly and shorter intraday time periods to fine-tune my entry to get in as early as possible with a low dollar risk.

You keep using the word *confirmation*. Would you give some example of how you determine that there is confirmation?

That's a good question. Everything I do in the market is oriented toward finding an edge. To me an edge is something I can go back into the past and see that it has happened 30 or 40 times. If I can say 7–9 times out of 10, when this has occurred it's happened following the bottom of a primary cycle, that would be a confirmation.

If during a particular time of year, 70 percent of the time when price has exceeded the previous week's high the bottom has held, then I can use that as a confirmation. It's not a sure thing; there are no sure things. But it puts the odds in my favor that I have that bottom.

Didn't you write a book about these confirmation tools?

The Power of Oscillator/Cycle Combinations. That fine-tunes it even more.

What kinds of oscillators are you talking about?

Many oscillators come into play as a quick scan. I don't use just one because sometimes they'll get out of whack. I modify the common oscillators (such as with a moving average or a detrend) so when price turns, the oscillator turns. I explain all that in the book.

One oscillator that I keep consistent is Stochastics. I don't change that. I just use different time frames. The problem with Stochastics is that it can get nailed to the floor or stuck to the ceiling during a strong move. If you're looking for a bottom, Stochastics isn't necessarily the best oscillator to use. Three oscillators I prefer are a modified RSI, Commodity Channel Index, and the 3-minus-10 moving average.

Russell Wasendorf

Another unique trend-following methodology belongs to Russell Wasendorf.

Russ, is trading with the trend important in your approach?

I don't know any principle that's more important than trading with the trend. As far as my personal trading is concerned or the trading recommendations that I make, all of them are an attempt to stick with the trend of the market. Determining that trend is perhaps one of the most difficult procedures.

In my analysis technique, I start from a macro position. I look at the index I have constructed to determine what the overall trend of all the markets is. I have a composite index I designed to determine the trend of the leading physical commodities. Twenty-one markets are represented in this index. By observing the index I attempt to determine whether or not the tide is rising or falling. All the boats in the harbor will rise if the tide is coming in. If the tide is going out, the boats in the harbor will all drop. I want to see the big picture.

This is based on Charles Dow's early research that he did around the turn of the century. He constructed his 13-market stock index, which eventually evolved into the Dow Jones Industrial Average. I use the same basic technique that he used to construct the Wasendorf Composite Index.

Once I have observed the overall trend of the market, I try to isolate what market groupings are having the greatest impact on the overall trend. I have four subindexes: a Grain Index, a Meat Index, a Metals Index, and a Food and Fiber Index. These give me a picture of the major market groups of the physical commodities.

Russell Wasendorf

Russell R. Wasendorf is currently president and chief executive officer of PFG, Inc., an Omnibus FCM, and president of Wasendorf & Son Company, an introducing brokerage firm. He is registered with the NFA as a commodity trading advisor (CTA) and as a commodity pool operator (CPO).

Wasendorf has authored or co-authored five books, including: *Commodity Trading—The Essential Primer*, *All About Futures*, *All About Commodities*, and *All About Options*. He has published a weekly market letter since 1980 (*Futures & Options Factors*) and a weekly chart service since 1984 (*Pocket Charts*).

Wasendorf was public affairs manager with the American Soybean Association from 1972 to 1976, and director of The Commodities Education Institute (CEI), a division of *Futures* magazine, from 1976 to 1980. In 1980 he established Wasendorf & Associates, Inc., a futures market research firm, and he founded the Center for Futures Education in 1981.

Born February 25, 1948, an Iowa native, he has a Bachelor of Arts degree from the University of Northern Iowa, where he was elected president of the honors program and senator of the student council.

Mr. Wasendorf is married and has one son.

The headquarters for his operation is 802 Main Street, Cedar Falls, IA 50613. Phone (319)-277-5240.

I observe not only the technical characteristics of the index itself. I also make a ratio comparison with the Wasendorf Composite Index to see how well the individual index is performing against the overall index.

I then look at what I call the internal character of each market. I observe how well the market is currently performing compared to how it has recently performed. I compare whether or not it is rising faster than it has risen before, is declining faster, or has maintained a level performance relative to recent history or longer-term history. Viewed in this light I get some idea of whether or not it has what I call internal strength within the trend.

The next part of the procedure is to compare the individual markets within the subindexes to the subindex itself. In the case of grains I would look at how well soybeans are performing within the Grain Index, how well corn is performing within the Grain Index, and so forth.

I look for leader and laggard characteristics. Leadership characteristics determine which markets are propelling the trend and laggard characteristics give me an indication of those markets that may be the next to move within the overall group.

Sometimes one market within a group is detrimentally affected by the uptrending characteristics of another. For example, if the soybean market is rallying very strongly, it might actually have a detrimental effect on the corn market, since soybeans have dominated the market group's buying pressure.

Usually, however, markets move in concert, and that's the whole point of using an index analysis procedure. By observing this step-by-step procedure, I try to isolate whether or how much a market is trending. As Dow described it, look at the tide, the waves, and the ripples.

It makes for some interesting analysis, but how does it actually affect your trading?

If commodities in general are rising, then the uptrends tend to be stronger, tend to have more staying power, and are more likely to continue for longer periods of time. All analysis relates to confidence—confidence and willingness to take a position. If the overall trend of the market is up, I will not only isolate the markets that are moving in concert with that trend, I will be a buyer of those markets. It also gives me confidence to diversify within a market group.

What if in the corn market the trend isn't really up; it's slightly down or sideways? Are you going to take a long position in the corn market just because everything else is strong? Or are you going to wait for corn to turn up?

There are two parts to this analysis. One is to determine the trend. Second, I have certain triggering mechanisms to enter a trade that include money management concepts.

Trend is only relevant in a particular time frame. What time frame do you use for the major trend?

Originally, because of the tax laws, I tried to isolate trends that were six months or longer. Because of the change in the tax laws abolishing the distinction between long- and short-term capital gains, trends do not hold as long as they used to.

Most trends in the markets, even strong momentum trends, last for only about nine months. So you have to enter that trend as early as possible. This requires finding early indications of reversals or trend changes. A trend change signal might be something as simple as breaking through a long-term down trendline. You cannot absolutely determine the duration of the new trend, but you have a good likelihood of getting into a long-term trend if you're looking at the broader scope of the market.

Do you look at daily, weekly or monthly charts?

All three.

If you're looking for a long-term trendline to be broken, would you accept something that happened on a daily chart, or would you require it to be on a weekly or monthly chart?

This reflects levels of confidence. You can take early positions based on very short-term trend changes. As a matter of fact, my initial procedure is to take positions based on such short-term trend changes. You build confidence and add positions as the trend moves through longer-term trendlines.

There are two considerations. One is a strict technical system procedure to establish a position. The second is what is going to be the size of that position. My positions will get larger based on my personal confidence.

What's the time frame of the shortest indicator that you'd use to take a position?

A simple close over a trendline on a daily chart is adequate to trigger a position.

TREND UNIMPORTANT

Craig Solberg

Some traders find trend totally unimportant. A good example is weather trader Craig Solberg.

Craig, you pretty much ignore trend in your trading, don't you?

Trading with the trend is not a factor we consider. Our forte is trading weather markets. In a weather market situation you will have a market that is going in a trend because of weather considerations. Let's take an example where the market is rising very quickly on those weather fears. You can trade with that bull trend as long as the weather forecast is in your favor. But there's going to be a morning when you walk into the office and the weather forecast has dramatically changed. Now it's the opposite of what caused the bull market. In 1988, we had huge moves in the soybean market due to dry weather. One day the forecast suddenly told us there was an excellent chance for rainfall across a good portion of the cornbelt. I was willing to buck the major trend on the very day the new weather forecast came out. I took a short position and managed to catch the top of that market.

From our perspective, it's fine to trade the trend as long as the weather forecast is in your favor. But you also must be aware that there can be a dramatic change from a bull trend to a bear trend when the weather forecast reverses. You really cannot trade the current trend when the weather forecast is no longer in your favor.

If somebody were conservative, they could decide to trade with weather information but only when it's in the direction of an established trend.

That's definitely a conservative way to play it. If the weather forecast is bullish, only enter a market if it is in an uptrend. If the market is in a downtrend but the weather forecast is bullish, you would wait for the market

Craig Solberg

Craig Solberg grew up on a farm in northeast Iowa before enrolling in the meteorology program at Iowa State University in the fall of 1985. His four years at Iowa State included winning the Iowa State Forecasting contest in the spring of 1989. He received his Bachelor of Science degree in May 1989.

Solberg has been employed by Freese-Notis Weather since May 1989. His interest in commodity trading grew through his association with noted commodity trading advisor Jim Roemer, and he registered as a commodity trading advisor in July 1990.

One of his main roles is contributing long-range weather, crop, and commodity price forecasts for the *Trade Winds* newsletter, and providing weather and commodity information for hotline and other daily services provided by Weather Trades.

Write Craig at Freese-Notis/Weather Trades, 2411 Grand Avenue, Des Moines, Iowa 50312. Phone: (515)-282-0233. Fax: (515)-282-6832. E-mail: trades@weather.net. WorldWide Web: http://www.weather.net.

to change trend before buying. In our opinion, it really depends on how substantial the forecast is to a particular crop region.

Larry Williams

Trading legend Larry Williams has a somewhat unique perspective on trend following.

Larry, in your kind of trading the trend is less important. What is your criticism of the concept "trade with the trend"?

I think it's inappropriate for short-term traders. In a large bull market the

Larry Williams

Larry Williams, now 52 years old, was the first "big name" in commodities—one of the innovators who popularized these markets in the 1960s. The best selling *How I Made One Million Dollars Trading Commodities* was Larry's first book. He also wrote the first book analyzing the seasonality of commodities, *Sure Thing Commodity Trading*. Other financial books by Williams include *The Secret of Selecting Stocks for Immediate and Substantial Gains* and *How Seasonal Factors Influence Commodity Prices*. Larry's latest work in the commodity field is *The Definitive Guide to Commodity Trading, Volumes One and Two*.

Larry has also authored a handful of books on other topics. *How to Prosper in the Coming Good Years* came out in 1982 and correctly forecast the largest surge of economic growth America has ever seen. On religion and law, there is *The Mountain of Moses*, an account of his clandestine trip to Saudi Arabia and documentation of a discovery of what appears to be Mt. Sinai; and *How to Outfox the Foxes*, a practical text that describes how to beat lawyers at their own game.

Every month Williams publishes two popular newsletters: *Commodity Timing* and *Treasure Hunter Confidential*.

More than an author, Larry astounded the commodity world in 1987 by parlaying $10,000 into over $1,100,000 in the 12-month Robbins World Cup Trading Championship. This is a feat and record that no trader has since been able to come close to matching.

Williams served on the board of the National Futures Association, representing fellow commodity trading advisors. Twice he ran for United States Senate in his home state of Montana, narrowly losing the general election by a few percentage points.

Write to Larry Williams at P.O. Box 8162, Rancho Santa Fe, CA 92067. Phone (800)-800-8333 or (619)-756-0421.

short-term trader will have some big-time, slam-down days. Of course, you should be a short seller on those days.

In bear markets there are sometimes huge 50- or 60-point rallies in the Dow in one day. And the next day it's right back down again. Certainly, when the market opened that morning, the short-term trend was down, the long-term trend was down, the intermediate-term trend was down. Every trend was down. But you can make a lot of money going against the trend on those days.

A short-term trader who thinks about trading only with the trend is not going to be as successful. You can't disallow those countertrend trades. You cannot walk away from buy signals because the market's been down or sell signals because the market's been up. Trading with the trend should be another separate strategy.

Wouldn't you say those comments apply mainly to the stock indexes, which are the worst trending markets on the board?

No. All markets have short-covering rallies in bear markets and bear raids in bull markets. Those are some of the most explosive one- or two-day moves there are. I'm looking at a coffee chart right now. Coffee was in a pretty good uptrend going into September 20, 1993. It had a huge down day on September 21st. Yet the trend was clearly up.

How do you identify those kinds of things that come out of nowhere?

I can't always identify them in advance. I just know I've made a lot of money selling short in bull markets and going long in bear markets. You can identify them with patterns, volatility breakouts, whatever techniques you're using. But don't put a filter in your trading that says, "The trend is up. I can't take any sell signals."

CONCLUDING THOUGHTS

Jack Schwager

For some concluding thoughts I turn to one of the most respected analysts and authors in the business, Jack Schwager.

Jack Schwager

Jack Schwager is currently director of Futures Research and Trading Strategy at Prudential Securities. He formerly held similar positions at Paine-Webber and Smith-Barney and has 22 years of experience heading up futures research departments. He is also a commodity trading advisor and one of the coprincipals of Wizard Trading, which began trading client money in September 1990 and currently has $33 million under management.

Schwager is the author of the highly regarded *A Complete Guide to the Futures Markets,* published by John Wiley & Sons in 1984; the best-selling *Market Wizards,* published by the New York Institute of Finance in 1989; and the equally popular *The New Market Wizards,* published by HarperCollins in 1992. Two other books, *Fundamental Analysis* and *Technical Analysis,* are scheduled for publication in 1995 as part of John Wiley & Sons' *Schwager on Futures* series. His work has also been incorporated in various anthologies and published in a variety of trade periodicals.

Schwager is a frequent seminar speaker and has lectured on a range of analytical topics with a particular focus on the characteristics of great traders, technical analysis, and trading system evaluation. He holds a B.A. in Economics from Brooklyn College and an M.A. in Economics from Brown University.

Jack, how critical is it to trade with the trend?

I used to think it was absolutely critical to success. That's still true for me and most other traders. Speaking for myself, since I'm the type that's not comfortable trading countertrend, trading with the trend is essential. In fact, most of the profitability from the strategy that I have devised comes out because of trends. The other elements are there just for protection when trends are not operating.

I've also come to understand that there are people who use completely countertrend-type methodologies and yet are quite successful. It's really a matter of style and personality. There are individuals who are oriented towards trading with the trend and are comfortable doing it that way. There are individuals whose personalities are oriented to quite the opposite, trading countertrend. A person has to discover which type he or she is. Most people will find it easier to trade with the trend than countertrend. It is possible to do it either way. It depends on the person and, of course, the methodology he or she derives.

What do you say to the argument that these supposed countertrend people are really trend traders trading with a shorter-term trend? Maybe they're trying to anticipate the next trend rather than wait for it to be established.

You do get into a bit of semantics here. I guess you could say there's always a trend at each moment. If you get down to five minutes, you're trading the five-minute trend. But I think that's misleading.

We're really looking at the style. Is the style a countertrend style or is it a trend style? By countertrend style I mean a style that looks for moves to be exhausted or showing signs of being exhausted anticipating that the rubber band will snap back the other way. Of course, by implication they're trading with the short-term trend back, but they're really trading the turning points. That's the key.

If the methodology is using prior movement and trading in the same direction as the prior movement, whether the prior movement is one week, one day, or 10 minutes, you can call it a trend methodology. If the methodology is looking at the prior movement and trying to define when that prior movement has run its course, when it's time to go the other way, then philosophically you're dealing with a countertrend methodology. That definition would hold up no matter what time spectrum you're dealing with.

The people you're talking about who are countertrend traders—are they actually trading before the market turns?

They're trying to catch the market turns.

How much confirmation do they need?

Typically they'll require some minor confirmation, but not enough to define any type of trend for someone like me. The move they're looking for is so short-term that to require any meaningful confirmation would miss the move they're trying to trade. They won't necessarily buy into a straight falling market.

They'll probably want to see some signs of stabilization and the market beginning to come back. There should be some evidence, some minor confirmation, but not enough to signify a change in the trend for a typical trend follower.

For example, if you want to think of it in terms of a physical analogy, think of a water fountain. The velocity of the water is great enough to exceed the force of gravity up to a certain point. There's a fine balance point at the peak of the arc where gravity equals the upward water power. Then the water starts coming back down.

These countertrend traders are trying to get the water on the way down. They're not shorting it while the stream is going up, but they're selling it somewhere near that upper arc point. Of course, they could be wrong a lot of times, in which case they'll be out quickly.

You think this is mostly a matter of personality. If you had to advise someone who seemed to be open minded, would you say it's better to be a trend follower like you are or a countertrend trader?

What I think it's better to be is what fits their personality. You can't force one into the other. Certain people are basketball players and certain people are jockeys. That obviously depends on a physical trait, namely height. It's the same thing in trading, although not as obvious. You can't look at somebody and say this person would be a better trend follower and this person would be a better countertrend trader. It's something each person has to discover himself or herself.

Just like a six-foot-ten person would be better off to pursue basketball as opposed to horse racing, the same analogy would apply in trading. There are certain people whose very nature is oriented to one style or the other. It's like saying categorically all people who pursue professional sports should be basketball players. That's nonsense. It's only those people who have the attributes. In the case of trading, they have to discover that for themselves.

Don't you think it's a lot more difficult to be a countertrend trader?

Yes, it is more difficult. It's more difficult for me because I'm not oriented to countertrend trading. I would find it very difficult. But if you speak to someone whom I would define as a countertrend trader, for them trying to trade with the trend is a difficult experience, while trading countertrend is quite natural.

Most people are attracted to picking tops and bottoms because it's perceived that the risk is lower. If you say that whatever people want to do is okay, aren't you enticing them into trying to do something that's more difficult than most people can manage?

Yes. I agree that most people will not be able to do it, but I have met individuals who were very comfortable trading countertrend. That's their style. Some markets actually are better to trade that way. Stock indexes are really better suited to a countertrend trader than they are to a trend trader. So what's difficult and what's not difficult depends somewhat on the nature of the market and the nature of the person. For most people who try to be countertrend traders, they're not apt to be successful.

I'm talking about someone who has developed a methodology that has some sort of edge in defining when a trend has run its course and who has an accompanying risk-control method to prevent being blown out when he or she is wrong. I'm not talking about people who scratch their head and think, "This market looks like it's turning down now, so I'm going to sell it." That would be a recipe for disaster.

Let's go back to you and your trend-following approach. In what time frame do you prefer to trade? Do you like to use weekly charts, daily charts?

Using subjective decision making—in other words, not a computerized system—I would start with a long-term chart and then go down to a daily chart. Occasionally I use an intraday chart, but usually just a daily. I would like to have a feeling for the direction of the major trend. It tends to be very long term. I may have a multiyear opinion on the market and trade around that opinion.

If you are looking at a weekly chart, how would you determine the trend based on the weekly chart?

I look more at patterns than magnitude of trend. A lot of it is judgment. When I read a chart, I'm looking for markets that don't behave in the way they're supposed to. I seek out various types of what I call failure signals. That's an important item. Breakouts that are sustained are reasonable signals. They need to be sustained because breakouts are so frequent that if you just follow all breakouts, you're not going to make money.

If the market comes down to a bottom and you're going to play an upside breakout, how long do you want the congestion pattern to take before the breakout?

There are no set rules. The longer the market moves sideways and the narrower the channel, the more significant a breakout is. The longer that breakout holds above the prior trading range, the more significant it is. Volatility increasing at the same time is significant. I don't know if I can spell it out in an entire formula. If I could, I wouldn't do it anyway.

Once you've established a trend on the weekly chart, are you satisfied that's the trend or do you also want to see some kind of confirmation on the daily?

I may decide that the trend has changed on the daily chart before I see it on the weekly. I like to look at a weekly chart first for a broader opinion. It may very well be that the daily chart will give me a signal first.

There is a problem with weekly charts unless you're looking at continuous charts, because so many weekly charts are tremendously distorted. I will give you a wonderful example. If someone is not convinced of the pitfalls of using continuation charts without being aware of what their drawbacks are, this would convince them of the danger. Most people won't appreciate it because they don't follow the foreign markets, but the foreign interest rate markets have become really big markets.

It's fascinating to look at the Euromark chart over the last nine months or so. Specifically, if you look at the weekly Euromark chart, what you see is a wonderfully uptrending market. There is upswing, consolidation, upswing, consolidation, upswing. A very constructive looking chart. If you look at a daily chart, on the other hand, what you see is a huge, broad, rounding top pattern—very negative. For some time the daily chart has been screaming bearish, while the weekly chart has been screaming bullish.

In this case I've been ignoring the weekly chart entirely for the simple reason that on the weekly chart, every three months when the contract expires you have a huge gap between the nearby and the forward. There is this nonexistent or what I call phantom price move from the nearby to the forward. What you see is upswings, but they are nothing more than contract transitions. That may tell you something about what the price level of the Euromark has been, but it certainly doesn't tell you what a trading position has done.

For a trading position you would have to look at either a continuous (not perpetual) price series that would remove those gaps or individual contracts. So theoretically I like to look at the weekly chart but often it may be the daily chart that is the deciding factor.

Do you use the same patterns on the daily charts that you talked about on the weekly?

Yes. I don't make a distinction between daily and weekly charts. I look at them the same way. I like to look for consolidation patterns and so forth. So the types of patterns I look at on the dailies are the same types of patterns I would look at on the weekly. If I was looking at an intraday chart, I would look at it the same way.

Will trading with the trend continue to work in the future?

The most direct way to profit in the market is to have a way to exploit the trend. That is where most of the money is. For most people, finding a way to extract the trend is going to be the only way to be successful.

Having said that, it's become more difficult to do because as trend following became more popular during the 1970s and 1980s, the markets have become choppier. The trends are still there, but they have become much more volatile and difficult to follow. Whatever trend-following techniques people come up with, they will be subject to periods of extreme drawdown. Trend following is going to become more difficult. The trick will become to extract the profits from trends and yet have other strategies to protect against that increased volatility.

I take it from that you think that always-in-the-market systems will be worse than ever.

Yes, I would say so. I'll put it this strongly. It's impossible to develop a single always-in-the-market, trend-following system that will not leave one vulnerable to some very severe periodic retracements.

What do you mean by "very severe"?

Drawdowns that are in line with the annual percentage return you're making. If you're trying to make 40 percent a year, then the drawdowns would be 40 percent a year.

Wouldn't that be about twice what the optimal drawdown is likely to be for an excellent system?

For a system to be good, a return of double the drawdown in percentage terms would be the minimum. My goal is an annual return of three times the maximum drawdown as a percentage of capital. Time will tell if I succeed in that.

That would be a very exceptional system, don't you think?

My approach is not one system. It's a combination of various kinds of strategies. No single strategy will do that for you.

I hope these experts have stimulated some thoughts for your own trend trading. In the next chapter, I'll use the same process to examine the concept of cutting losses short.

CHAPTER 3

Cut Losses Short

Strictly speaking, cutting losses short is an ingredient of managing risk. However, it is so important to successful trading that it deserves its own separate category. The decision of how to cut losses if a trade does not work out should be a key element of the trade selection process for every trade. However, the trader can make the decision of how to escape from a losing trade in many different ways.

The experts we interviewed had numerous ways of cutting losses short. They can be roughly divided into the following categories: chart-based stops, indicator stops, entry method stops, volatility stops, money management stops, margin-based stops, and account equity stops.

CHART-BASED STOPS

By chart-based stops we mean placing stops at some point of significance on a bar chart. This may be in reference to a chart pattern, a trendline, or a pivot point that represents support or resistance.

Bill Gary

Bill Gary is an expert on fundamental analysis. He recognizes the importance of technical analysis in the decision-making process as well.

Bill, how important is the principle of cutting losses short to successful trading?

It's important to give yourself enough latitude to let the trade work. I never place my stops extremely close when I'm entering a position. I'd rather take a small position and give myself plenty of latitude in the initial stages of a move to let that market work. Once it does begin to perform, then I start looking at different ways I can reduce the risk and bring the stop closer.

It sounds like you take issue with the statement because you're worried about the word *short*. **That implies you don't want to use a small stop. What about restating the principle as just cutting your losses. You don't have a problem with that, do you?**

Absolutely not.

How important is it?

It's critical. It's the only thing that will keep you in the game. The long-term objective is to stay in the game. It doesn't make any difference what I might think or what anybody thinks if the market is going against you.

How do you decide where to place your initial stop?

I usually place my initial stop for long positions below major support. For short positions, it would be above major resistance. I take a small original position. Normally, my greatest risk exposure is going to be during the initial stages of a move.

How much are you willing to risk?

I let the market tell me.

How do you define major support or resistance?

A major bottom or top. I look at the daily and weekly charts and look for a major support area or a major top.

You're using a chart-based stop.

Yes.

Do you always use a chart-based stop?

Yes.

Glen Ring

Glen Ring is editor of the *Trends in Futures* newsletter.

Glen, how important is cutting losses short?

It is perhaps a buzzword phrase in commodity trading. At the same time, it is also as close mechanically to *the* key as anything. About five years ago I consciously started the process of studying trading rather than just studying the markets. In studying winning traders and trading myself, one of the things I've become very aware of is that cutting losses short is of the utmost importance.

Here are some examples from my own trading. I had a recent month where I made eight trades. There were seven winners and one loser, and yet I was a net loser for the month. On all the seven winners I ended up with small profits after transaction costs. The one loser hit my maximum allowable risk, and it wiped out all my winners.

Another time I closed seven losers in a row. But the eighth trade put me at a new equity high for the year. This shows how important it is to have a small loss, a small loss, a small loss. You hear the Tommy Baldwins, the Richard Dennises of the world claim to make all their profits on 5 or 10 percent of their trades. It's like being a boxer where you punch, punch, punch all night long hoping to land one or two or three knockout punches.

Having those small losses is what keeps you in the game, keeps you in position for when you do catch a trend or a big move. But it's a law of numbers to me. If I can make enough controlled-loss trades, even a blind squirrel is going to find a nut once in a while.

How small is small?

Ah, that's very important. That's something you have to define for your own situation. The vast majority of people overtrade their equity tremendously. The people that try to trade with $5,000 or $10,000 are trading with at least one hand tied behind their back already. But small is a relative term. I like to think of it in terms of percentages. I think that if you're limiting your risk on individual trades to one to two percent of your trading equity, that would be ideal. When you're trading with smaller equities such as $20,000 on down, you have to accept a higher percentage of risk in most instances. But to exceed five percent would put most people on an eventual suicide mission.

That gives you the potential for a lot of losses in a row without doing too much damage.

Absolutely. Anybody who's been in this business for any length of time recognizes that they could easily have a string of losses, maybe approaching 10 losses in a row. You may have a breakeven thrown in there or some very small profits. You can easily go 10 trades in a row without catching a big winning trade. You may have some stress in your life or the markets may not be in an ideal trading environment.

If you're a purely mechanical trader, you can run into some very bad stretches of nontrending market activity. If you test across the physical commodities, you'll find that 1989 was a killer for most trend-following models.

If you have 10 losers in a row and you're risking not over 2 percent of your equity, you're only going to have a 20 percent drawdown after 10 consecutive losses. Most people can handle a 20 percent drawdown and still keep following their rules. Those people who are risking 5 or 6 percent of their equity on each trade all of a sudden are down 50 or 60 percent. They lose their perspective. They will find it hard to go through the trading process with a clear frame of mind.

How do you decide personally where to put your stops?

It's defined by the market. If I'm trading a pure trend-following pattern, then I'll place the stop beyond the reaction lows or reaction highs. I've tested various markets for what is the proper amount beyond those reactions. I've found that you're going to get stopped out of some trades due to market noise, if you want to call it that. I use mostly four ticks, four minimum price moves beyond those extremes. Sometimes I get stopped out on the high or low of the day, but there are also times I get missed by a tick or two. I've found that is as close as I can possibly bring it and still give the market adequate room.

There are any number of ways to place stops. It's less important how you do it than it is to define your rules in advance and apply them consistently.

What do you do if your chart stop is too big for your equity?

I don't take the trade.

You pass the trade rather than manipulate the stop or the entry?

Absolutely. Pass the trade. My number one objective right now, what I'm striving towards, is great defense. I go back to the 1985 Chicago Bears when they made the play-offs. They shut out the Rams, and they shut out the Giants. As long as they weren't letting the other teams score on them, they could play all day and not lose. We've seen any number of sporting teams with great offenses, but they usually go down in flames once they run into the great defenses. They haven't developed their defense to stop the periods of what you might call drawdowns.

My number one rule is to protect the capital I already have. My number two rule is to protect any open equity I may have. My number three rule is to try to make profits. I define my trades first by determining what is my risk. If my risk doesn't fit the parameters for my account, the trade doesn't go on.

This opens up another issue. I saw an example yesterday of an account that somebody was promoting trading $20,000. There were three contracts of soybeans on, a couple of contracts of corn, a contract of cattle, and another contract of this or that. I quickly calculated the risk. In soybeans alone the risk was about 12 percent of the entire account. That to me is suicide. You're betting on being right, not betting on the law of numbers being on your side.

Let's say I'm willing to accept a maximum of 3 percent equity risk per trade on a $20,000 account. That's only $600. I see a potential soybean trade where the risk has to be 30 cents. That's $1,500 for a full-sized contract. Many people are so macho they won't look at the Mid-America Exchange as an alternative.

Last year I did pretty well trading interest rate futures. With the exception of only one trade, they were all in Mid-Am bonds. That was on the model account, which is a $10,000 account. What I'm saying is there are ways to manage your risk. If your stop number is bigger than what your account will accept, either look for another vehicle to make the trade or pass it.

Peter Brandt

Peter Brandt is a long-time professional trader and editor of *The Factor*. He specializes in trading classical chart patterns.

Peter, what is your philosophy on cutting losses short?

I absolutely believe in cutting losses short. I don't have much tolerance for a loss any greater than $300 a contract. For me there are two components to a trade: the direction of a market and the timing for entry. I may be right on the direction, but if I'm not right on the timing, the trade's not right. If I'm losing $300 or $400 on a trade, I've got to say to myself that my timing wasn't right.

It's really important to me to be able to keep coming back to the markets each day. In most businesses if you run out of inventory, you're out of business. The only thing a trader has is his capital. A trader's capital, his account equity, is his inventory. It's extremely important to keep that inventory intact. That's why I do not believe in letting losses go against me very far.

Using such small stops, you have to put up with a fairly low percentage of accuracy.

There is definitely a tradeoff. Some people emotionally can't handle any approach where they're wrong more than 20 or 30 percent of the time. Using tight stops you have to be willing to trade over an extended period and be right only 30 or 40 percent of the time.

What kind of stops do you use? How do you pick them?

I base them on chart points—highs and lows of either chart patterns or individual days.

You don't use money management stops.

No.

Or volatility stops.

No. That's something I played with, but I don't use them. Most really good trades that I've had over the years have gone my way right away and have never looked back. So tight stops have not jeopardized the best trades I've had. I would guess that very few of my biggest trades have gone against me more than $200 or $250.

Do you still use the Last Day Rule?

Yes.

Would you describe that?

Once I've drawn the parameters of a classical chart pattern (such as a triangle or head and shoulders) and I have the boundary lines, I will use the opposite extreme of the last day in which the market traded within the pattern as a base point to establish a stop price. In the case of an upside breakout from the pattern, it would be the low of the last day the market traded within the pattern. In the case of a downside breakout from the pattern, it would be the high of the last day the market traded within the pattern.

Craig Solberg

Craig Solberg is editor of *Trade Winds*. A weather trader, he uses a different kind of chart stop that involves retracements of previous price swings.

Craig, how would you rate cutting losses short among the four cardinal principles?

Of your four principles, this is the one to which I try to adhere most stringently. You have to get into the market on your terms. A good axiom to remember is that it's better to be out of the market wishing you were in, than in the market wishing you were out.

I don't like to buy a market at any price. I'd rather have it come back to me, so I can get in at a price where I can manage the trade. I get in at this price. I'm going to risk to this level. I'm going to take profits at that level.

How do you decide where to put your stops?

My favorite way is to use retracements. Many times I'll look for a 50 percent retracement level of a particular upmove to enter. I'll then risk that trade to the 62° percent retracement level. Another method I like is if you are buying a market above a gap, you risk to the point where the market would fill that gap.

As weather traders, a key factor in placing stops is our confidence in the forecast. If we're confident enough about the forecast, we're going to risk a looser stop on the position because our profit potential is very good. I like to use a three-to-one reward/risk ratio. For example if I'm trying to make 30 cents in soybeans, I'll risk about a dime on that position.

You mentioned that you prefer chart-type stops. But sometimes do you use money management stops, too?

You try to blend the two together. First of all, you calculate your profit potential on the trade. Say it's 30 cents. So you'd want to risk somewhere around 10 cents. Then you look at the chart patterns. You look at potential retracements and see if there is a level where the risk is about 10 cents. We're trying to get a good reward/risk ratio and also risk to a good technical support area on the price charts.

Phyllis Kahn

Phyllis Kahn is a pure Gann trader who tries to enter right near significant tops and bottoms.

Phyllis, how important is cutting losses in your style of trading?

It's very important. I don't think one should ever be in the market without an open protective stop. Ever. You should be quick to take losses if the trade doesn't materialize. You may have to reinstitute the trade in the event that the market goes back in your favor, but in the meantime you're stopped out.

Because you enter so close to the extreme, does that mean your stop automatically goes just beyond the extreme before your entry?

I enter when the market goes a particular number of points above the previous day's high (for long positions) in my trend-change time window. I place my stop the same number of points below the low. For example, in the S&P it would be 40 points below the low.

The same confirmation you require over the previous day's high for entry you subtract from the low for your stop.

Yes. That's my way of doing it. There are people who follow the Gann trend-change dates and use an entirely different method. But this has been very successful for me.

What's the reason you just don't put it one tick below the low? If the low is going to be taken out, aren't you wrong?

Yes, but there is a certain amount of noise in that area, too. I don't think one tick is ever sufficient either for entry or exit. You have to give yourself some room, but you must also limit risk.

Is that also because other stops are probably there?

Yes.

Isn't there some danger that with all the stops that are going to be there, you're going to be filled 40 points lower than you would have otherwise?

Sure there is some danger of that, but you'd be surprised how seldom it happens, especially if it's a momentum reversal, which most of them are. They come down hard and then turn around and take out the previous day's high. You don't see that kind of reversal fail very often. It happens, but it's not a frequent occurrence.

If that's so, then having the stop one tick below the low wouldn't make any difference, would it?

It might not. I'd have to go back and study it, but there's no reason to put it that close. The following day you can move it. Once your position is profitable at today's close, tomorrow you can put it just a little bit below today's close and you're locking in a profit. Once you have a nice profit, you don't even have to go below the low of the previous day.

It's the old cliche, "Don't let a winning trade become a losing trade." Any time you have a 200-point profit you should protect it, especially right after entry. Then if you get a really big spring for three or four days, you can be a little slower about trailing the stop up.

Is there any necessary relationship between the size of the loss that you're willing to take and your account size? You're putting your stop 40 points below the low in the S&P. What if that's a long way from your entry and creates a potential $2,000 loss? Do you have to look at what size your loss is in relation to your account? Does keeping your losses small mean anything in dollar terms?

Yes. You don't take the trade if you're not willing to put your stop below the low of the low day. You have to be willing to follow the rule of putting your stop below the low.

Is there any rule of thumb about what size of loss is too big for an account?

A person has to decide that individually for himself or herself.

It's a question of personal comfort rather than a percentage of your account?

Yes. There are some people who don't have the stomach to trade a big, fast market. For example, to trade soybeans when they're really hot—or silver. They shouldn't trade those markets, period, because they are too volatile. A person has to be comfortable with the losses his or her trading method may generate.

I also believe that if you have three losing trades in a row, you should stop trading for several weeks and try to analyze why you had those three losing trades.

That comes under risk management. Let's save that for a future chapter.

Tom Aspray

Tom Aspray is a currency expert and primarily a short-term trader.

Tom, how do you handle cutting losses short?

Since I follow the cash currency markets pretty closely and they are open 24 hours a day, that affects how I handle my trades. If I don't get my expected results on a trade and I have to sleep for four or five hours, I may take it off at breakeven or with a small loss. If, on the other hand, it has moved as I expected, then I'll usually move the stop in so it's fairly tight and leave it when I'm not watching the market.

How tight is tight?

Translating from cash to something futures traders understand, it's about 25 or 30 ticks in the U.S. dollar or the deutschemark.

That's about $300. How important is the principle of cutting losses short to successful trading?

In terms of absolute numbers, it's pretty important. Psychologically, it's even more important. Successful trading is some combination of expertise plus confidence. Most traders would admit that when they go through down periods in their equity curve, their confidence level decreases at the same rate. If you can limit losses, you can maintain more confidence. By keeping that confidence level higher, you should have a greater degree of success. The discipline to limit losses allows you to stay in the game and trade for a longer period of time.

If you're trading futures rather than cash, how do you determine your stops?

I usually base it on hourly chart analysis, Fibonacci retracements, and support and resistance levels. I use a combination of methods. If I can come up with a similar number using several different methodologies, then I have greater confidence in it.

So they will be chart-based stops primarily.

Yes. I also use some mathematical price projection analysis to determine daily pivot points. I calculate the day's expected high, expected extreme high, expected low, and expected extreme low, and I also use those numbers to assist in stop placement.

Walter Bressert

Walter Bressert trades based on cycles.

Walt, how important is it to cut your losses short?

You can't trade the market if you don't have the money. The only way you're not going to have the money is if you lose it. As speculators, part of our business is taking losses. We're all going to take losses probably 30–50 percent of the time. From that viewpoint you could say that controlling losses is even more important than trading with the trend. You can trade against the trend and still have a chance to make money, but you can't make money if you lose your capital. If you can keep your dollar risk small, you open yourself up for sizeable profits. That's extremely important.

How do you cut losses short in your style of trading?

Minimizing my losses, cutting them short, means that I've got to be in control. My approach to trading is always to be in control.

Let me talk a little bit here about something that really bothers me. When I talk to people who do not trade futures and tell them what I do, they often respond, "You're a gambler." I'm not a gambler. I have no desire to gamble. When I go to Las Vegas, I don't gamble at all.

I'm a speculator. Being a speculator means I can set the odds. I can decide when I'm going to enter the market. I can decide how I'm going to enter the market, and I can decide how I'm going to get out of the market. You can't do that when you gamble.

I can go back in history, study patterns, and set up odds that are in my favor. When I choose to enter the market, I know from my research that I have a good chance to make money. Whenever I get into a position, it is because price has completed a pattern and the market should continue in my direction for at least a short period of time.

I have a predetermined price level or stop that tells me when I'm wrong. I control my losses by always having a stop-loss order at that price level. And I always know how much I'm going to lose on a trade per contract.

In controlling my losses I start with the individual contract, and I move up to the total position. I don't like to risk much more than 5 percent of my equity on any total position. Depending on the market, it could be 2 to 3 percent. By strictly controlling my losses, I can be wrong many times and still survive to trade again.

How do you decide where to put your stops?

I'm dealing with cycles. Everything revolves around whether this is a cycle bottom or top for a particular time frame. When I buy a market, I put a sell stop below what should be that cycle bottom. If I'm buying a cycle bottom, the lowest price bar or swing low before my entry is going to be my stop-loss. If a shorter-term pattern develops after the bottom, the stop can change. It might be based on an intraday price level. But it's always a bottom. It's always a low price.

In other words, you use chart-based stops, and you pick the chart point in relation to the cycles that you're trading.

Yes. I use chart-based points for entry and exit. The most important thing to me is the price level. For example, there is a price level where the market should not go if the current trend is to continue. By taking out that price level, the market is indicating that the current trend is no longer in force, at least for awhile.

If the chart point that you want to use is so far away that it makes the risk too big, do you just pass the trade?

I either pass on the trade or I drop down to a smaller time frame that reduces my risk. In that case I would decrease my odds of being right, but lower my dollar risk if I'm wrong.

If the stop on the daily chart is too far away, you might try to use one on an hourly chart?

I'll drop down to an hourly chart or a 15- or 5-minute chart and look to enter using those. Once the market moves in my favor, I'll be able to adjust my stop accordingly.

Would you ever use a chart point on a weekly chart rather than the daily?

Absolutely. What I'm looking for more than anything else is certainty. There's no absolute certainty. I'm talking about determining a degree of certainty of whether I'll make money or lose money on the trade.

Weekly charts help me do that. For example, if I exceed a weekly high in my oscillator/cycle combination, I look for the oscillator and the market to drop lower. Then if the oscillator turns up and price exceeds the previous week's high, the high of that week becomes important. If price then exceeds that high, it tells me that the odds are very good that this market is going to continue higher.

If I'm using a weekly chart, my stop is going to be the previous low of the cycle which is often a week or two before entry, and that may make the risk too big. I'll have to look at daily and intraday charts to find a closer stop point. I use the weekly chart to determine that the cycle has turned and then use hourly or intraday prices to enter the market in the direction of the trend, sometimes a day or two later.

I'm always using chart patterns, previous price lows, and what I call overextended energy. I view the markets as energy. We can see this energy in cycles and oscillators. Everything I do combines cycles and oscillators. They're both time-related. When an oscillator is extremely oversold, often there is a cycle that is about to bottom as well. I can determine that from the time frame of the previous cycle low. If the oscillator and time match up, I know that the energy is such that this market is oversold. Even though it may not go up, it's not going to go down much. It's at least going to go sideways and perhaps up a little bit before it goes down. I look for extreme oversold levels for buying and extreme overbought levels for selling. I use the energy as the market springs from those levels to enter and also to take a quick profit.

If a cycle bottom is late, the market is going lower longer than it should. Does that deter you from taking a long position with the idea that maybe the downtrend is too extreme and you'd rather take a short position after the next cycle top?

Generally when I'm looking for a bottom, the market is oversold enough using weekly and daily oscillators that I don't want to go short. I like to go into a market where there's a lot of energy to move it in the direction I'm trading.

I wasn't saying you would go short at the bottom, but would you be nervous about taking a long position because there was so much more downside strength than you expected?

Yes. In that case I might look for not just a simple upturn but rather a bottom, an upmove, and then a retest before I would enter.

One of the patterns I use is the retest that is often necessary for picking bottoms. You don't necessarily want to try to pick the low week, the low day, or the low hour. You want to wait for a pattern coming up from those in one form or another. A successful retest is often a good sign.

A retest is an energy flow. The market has made a bottom, moved back up, and gone back down; it can't take out the low, and then it turns around and comes back up again. I look for that pattern retest in all time frames.

INDICATOR STOPS

By indicator stops, I mean a stop point that you set by virtue of an indicator such as a moving average or Momentum. It is not a chart stop because it is mathematically based. A volatility stop, discussed below, is a special kind of indicator stop.

Michael Chisholm

Michael Chisholm is editor of *Taurus,* which he has published since 1976.

Michael, how important is cutting losses short?

It's difficult to choose among any of your principles. It's analogous to trading being an automobile and each one of the principles being one of the tires. You might be able to get the car to move without one of them, but if any are missing, it's going to be a bumpy ride. The more you're missing, the bumpier the ride is going to be.

Cutting losses short is very important to my trading. I predetermine my initial stop placement before I ever enter a trade. I do this as a result of computer testing—nonoptimized as much as possible.

You want your stops close enough to cut losses short, but you don't want them so close you get chopped up. That's a difficult thing to do. I've come up with some ideas from looking at charts on the computer screen that fall flat on their face when tested historically.

I take a basket of 10 commodities that represent all the commodities in the marketplace. I test over 10 years of data on these 10 commodities. I try every kind of initial protective stop with a number of variables for each method on all 10 of the markets. I total and average them out to find the one that seems to be the best for the whole basket of markets. Sometimes I use a straight dollar value, but the two I use most frequently are the value of a moving average and the value of a channel based on volatility.

Cutting losses short is a lot like locking in profits. It has to be purely mechanistic. The elements of fear and greed come into play so much, especially fear. There have been times when I've been tempted to move my stop farther away to stay with a promising position. Nine times out of 10 that doesn't work. The way my brain and most people's brains work is we tend to forget those nine times we were wrong but remember that one time when we were successful. Without a mechanical method, you let your emotions become involved. That can be dangerous.

How do you use the moving average as a stop?

Let's say I have a long position and am using a 30-day, simple moving average. Of course, the moving average has to be below the entry price to work, but with a trend-following system, it will be. Whatever the value of the moving average is on the day of entry, I place my initial protective stop there. I keep it there until another rule triggers me to begin moving the stop up to protect open profits.

The initial stop is fixed as of the time you enter the trade. You don't adjust it with the moving average as the trade develops?

Exactly.

You also mentioned a volatility channel. When using volatility do you

also keep your initial stop fixed until a different trailing stop rule takes over?

Right.

Do you pay any attention to the value of your account in terms of the amount to risk on a trade?

No, except from the standpoint of whether or not I'll take the trade at all. If I have, let's say, 95 percent of my account tied up in existing positions and I don't want to close any of them, and I have a potential trade that requires an initial stop greater than 5 percent of the account, I'll pass on the trade. I won't adjust the stop to the amount of money available in the account. That's a very poor practice.

How do you determine whether your account is used up? What do you measure?

I will only risk 5 percent of account value on any one trade. When 100 percent of the account is tied up, I don't take any more trades until something closes out.

ENTRY METHOD STOPS

By entry method stops, I mean some stop point that you set by virtue of your entry method. It may be a reverse entry signal or it may occur as a result of the violation of some or all of the trade's entry conditions.

Robert Miner

Robert Miner is editor of the *Major Market Analysis Report*. He has also authored a terrific trading course on Gann Methods.

Bob, how important is cutting losses short to your success as a trader?

Cutting losses is absolutely critical.

How do you do it?

I set my stops within the context of the methodology I use. The same methodology that says enter the trade has to tell you when the trade is wrong. You should determine your stop point before you enter a trade. It should be at the price where, if I were to enter, I would be on the wrong side of the market.

A further limitation is that the maximum capital exposure on any trade should not exceed 5 percent of the account equity. Once I determine my initial stop price, I look to see where is the farthest place I can enter without violating the 5 percent rule. If I can't enter within that range, then I can't take the trade. That may not be where I put my entry, but it is the limit.

If you're using projected turning points, how do they tell you where you are wrong?

Whatever method tells you that you're right also has to tell you that you're wrong. If a market exceeds the price and time projection windows, then the trade will be wrong. I have a two- or three-day time window and a four-day price zone. If price exceeds those, it tells me I should be out of the trade.

Could you give an example?

Sure. Take gold. Let's say between July 21 and 23 is a strong time projection. Let's say that between $380 and $383 is where the price projection is. That's a $3 price window. So if the market trades into that $380 to $383 price zone between July 21 and 23, there is a high probability for a trend change.

The trigger is a reversal signal. If the reversal signal occurs, then everything says the trend has changed. Your stop in that case is literally just one tick beyond the extreme of that day, because if it takes out that price, it's taking out the price zone and the time zone and the reversal signal. Everything you thought was right is now wrong, so you exit the trade and stand aside until the next setup.

That takes a lot of discipline to do, doesn't it?

Yes it does. There's a great potential for fudging.

How do you make your price projections?

I do both price and time projections in exactly the same way. They're ratios of previous retracements and projections of half swings.

You look at the time of the swing and the distance of the swing and then you project off that.

Both the time range and the price range.

Jake Bernstein

Jake Bernstein has written 27 trading books and has published his weekly market letter for over 20 years.

Jake, how would you rate cutting losses short among the four cardinal principles?

Cutting losses is one of the most important things you can do. May I tell a little story about what happened when I went to the Alabama Farm Bureau to give a speech?

Sure.

After I gave my speech they brought a fellow to meet me whom they claimed was the best pork belly trader in the entire state. He was an old guy, and he wanted to show me his trading system. Naturally, always wanting to learn another good system, I invited him to continue.

He reached into his pocket and pulled out a little velvet case with a pendulum inside. He asked me to open a chart book. He said, "Here's what you do. Hold the pendulum over the chart by the string until it stops swinging. That's the most important part of my system."

. . .This is a true story . . .

"When it stops swinging, steady it and then take your hand off and let it go. If it swings up and down, you buy. If it swings left and right, you sell."

I was impressed with the guy. He seemed like a wise old man who knew a lot about the markets. I asked if there was anything else I should know about the system.

He said, "Yes, there is one more thing, but it ain't too important."
I said, "What's that?"
"Well if what I buy or sell at the beginning of the day shows a loss at the end of the day, I kick it out."
"Is that it?"
"That's it."
What was he doing? He was keeping only his winners and getting rid of his losers fast.

This point about not holding any losers overnight, you hear that quite often. Is this to be taken literally? Do you really recommend that somebody never in their trading career go home with a loss? Isn't that going to give you too many losses? Too low a winning percentage?

I wouldn't recommend it without doing some thorough research in the context of the rest of the system. The market has enough of a random element so that on the first few days after you put on a good position, it could certainly close against you. But I'd say if by the end of the week at the very longest, a week after you put on a trade, it hasn't moved in your favor, the odds are pretty slim that it will turn out to be an exceptional trade.

In the phrase *cut losses short*, how short is short?

To me, that's a function of the system. Cutting losses short means getting out of your losers when your system says so. It doesn't mean to have a predetermined dollar amount at which to exit, although I do like the concept of an emergency stop-loss dollar amount that overrides everything else.

When you say your system, does this mean when you get a reversal signal?

Yes, or if the system is one that goes neutral, you exit at that point. In terms of research and trading, I have found that a stop-loss that is too tight guarantees you one thing. You will take a lot of losses and be a victim of the random aspects of the market.

So stop-losses can't be too tight, but that's a function of the system. In researching a couple of my day trading systems in the S&P, I found, for example, that the average profit per trade increased dramatically as the stop-loss was increased from 100 points to 500 points. Any individual looking at a 500-point stop-loss in the S&P for a day trade would say, "You've got to be crazy." On the other hand, my research said you would have to be crazy to use a 100-point stop.

Markets need room. You've got to give them room because no matter how much we may not want to admit it, market prices do have a random component. That random component will stop you out if your stop is too tight.

If you're using a big stop like that, don't you have to relate it somehow to your account size? Not every small account can be using $2,500 stops, can it?

I agree. Let's face it, there are thousands of traders out there day trading the S&P who ought not to be doing it. They can't afford the risk, and they can't give the market enough leeway within the boundaries of their small account size.

What kind of rule of thumb should there be for the relationship between your maximum stop size and your account size?

I don't think anyone who can't afford to risk at least $15,000 should be trading anything.

Does that mean the minimum to start is $15,000?

That's my opinion.

Could you trade with $2,500 stops with a $15,000 account?

You could, but you'd only be in the game a few times if you were wrong.

If somebody wanted to trade with $2,500 stops, what would you say the minimum account size should be?

I think you have to allow yourself the luxury of losing 10 times in a row. If you lose 10 times in a row at $2,500 a trade, that's $25,000. That's not at all unrealistic.

So you'd have to have the margin on top of that and be prepared to lose $25,000.

Correct.

You haven't mentioned anything about what is perhaps the most popular kind of stop—the chart stop. Have you discounted that as a stop placement method?

I don't think they work. Joe Granville used to say, "If it's obvious, it's obviously wrong." There's a lot of truth in that little epigram. Too many people do the obvious thing and say, "Let's try to put the stop at the low of the day." There are 10,000 other people thinking the same way. The odds are that approach is not going to work.

VOLATILITY STOPS

By volatility stops, I mean a stop placed using distance from entry calculated as some percentage of recent volatility. The percentage may be over or under 100 percent. You may measure volatility in a number of ways. In general, it is the vertical range of prices over some recent time period.

Stan Tamulevich

Stan Tamulevich is a short-term trader and editor of *Marketline Update*.

Stan, how important is the placement of initial stops to your trading?

It's the key to survival and the key to success. I'm not really looking for big moves. I use fairly tight stops. In fact, some people say they're too tight. I'm often stopped out with wash trades, breakeven-type trades. You've got to keep your potential losses smaller than profits. When you're looking at an average profit in the $300 range as I am, you must keep losses down near $100 if you can. It sounds like a difficult task, but I take advantage of every opportunity I have to put my stops very close to the market.

Do you use stops in the market? In other words, do you put your stop orders on the floor as opposed to using mental stops that you execute after the market has reached your price?

I don't use mental stops. It's too easy to let things get away from you.

How do you decide where to put your tight stops?

It's usually based on some factor of volatility. I'll look at the range for the last three or four days or even just the last day. If the market moves the distance of the previous day's range against me, I'm out of it. Usually, it's considerably less than that.

It's a volatility stop, but you don't mathematically calculate some average. You eyeball the chart and deduce it from there.

To an extent. My standard would be to look at half the previous day's volatility and consider that as the danger point.

How do you define volatility? Is it the high minus the low? Or would it be the true high minus the true low?

The high minus the low. An excursion beyond half of that would make me nervous about a position.

On the average, what size of a stop in terms of dollars does that lead to?

It's fairly small. It depends obviously on the market. In grains it would be just two or three cents.

Many people would say you're going to be taken out by the market noise. What do you say to them?

Very often I am. So what? If the bottom line works out, you can stand a little noise. I was taken out by some noise in the gold market yesterday. It turned out to be a very small loss, 40 cents. The market proceeded back up today, and I have no problem with that. I'm always willing to take a $40 loss.

One nice corollary to your methods is that you can do your kind of trading with a lot smaller account than most methods require. What's the minimum size account you think someone should have to trade like you do?

You can take all my trades with a $5,000 account.

That's quite unusual.

A person ought to have $10,000 or $15,000, but if you want to get your feet wet and have good discipline, with these kinds of stops you can trade and not anticipate big drawdowns.

We can see how somebody could be quite comfortable trading like you do with only a $5,000 account to start.

I'm definitely a minority case.

Russell Wasendorf

Russell Wasendorf is involved with most aspects of the futures industry. Since he uses volatility as his stop criterion and also reverses his position when stopped out, his stops can be considered both volatility stops and entry method stops.

Russ, how do you cut your losses short?

My trading procedure always involves a stop. As a matter of fact, I enter the market on stops. Therefore, I only enter a market when it has moved through a trigger level that stops me into the market.

The closeness of my protective stop is determined by the current volatility of the market. For instance, if soybeans are currently exhibiting a daily volatility of 15 cents, I'm going to put my stop outside that volatility so the market can make its noise. It can bounce within its normal volatility without stopping me into a reverse position.

If the volatility increases, would you move your stop further away?

No. The stop determination depends on historical volatility. It won't move further away from the market.

How important is the principle of cutting losses short to overall trading success?

It's extremely important. It's a matter of making sure you have marbles to play the game the next day. I would classify following the trend as the number one principle and cutting losses short as number two.

And yet, your methodology seems to be less concerned with keeping your losses small than it is with not getting shaken out of a potentially winning position. Would that be a fair statement?

That is a fair statement, although being shaken out of a position can happen if the market suddenly becomes more volatile. If I base my stop on historical volatility and suddenly tomorrow the market becomes more volatile, then I'll probably lose my position. I can always resume the position based on a new trigger that reestablishes the trend.

The triggering mechanism will not only stop me out of the market, it reverses my position. I'm either long or short all the time. I'll be shaken out if the market becomes more volatile, and I'll be shaken out of a long position in exchange for a very short-term short position. If the volatility remains relatively high, I'll probably end up back in the long position. There would be a whipsaw there, but the whipsaws are less of a concern so long as I have the opportunity to benefit from market movement regardless of its direction.

In terms of the statement, "Cut your losses short," you're less concerned with the short than you are with cutting losses. As long as you cut losses, you're apparently not that concerned with how big the loss is because you don't have any mechanism that regulates the size of the loss other than the volatility of the market.

Right. That's one of the sobering factors about the markets. If you try to dictate the precise level of risk tolerance, then your desired risk level may be incompatible with market conditions. I've always felt that I had to be well capitalized to trade in the first place. I like to allow the markets to set the positioning of my stops and not have capital restrictions or my psychology of loss tolerance interfere.

MONEY MANAGEMENT STOPS

By money management stops, I mean a stop based on a fixed dollar amount. While these stops are often criticized as not being market related, they do have several advantages. First, if the purpose of the stop-loss is to manage risk, a money management stop does that in the most direct way possible. Second, if you are concerned about collusion in the pits to pick off stops, money management stops do not go at obvious places where many other stops are (except occasionally by coincidence).

James Kneafsey

James Kneafsey has been a major money manager since 1977.

Jim, how important do you think cutting losses short is?

I put a great deal of premium on cutting losses. If you are in the market all the time and you keep your losses short, you should be profitable.

When you use small stops with an always-in-the-market system, you tend to have lots of losses.

That's true. It is why you have to make sure your commission rate and your slippage are very low. I'm not talking about $50 or $100 losses, but rather something in the $200 to $500 range.

Doesn't this require some experience to handle the psychological aspects of trading with a low percentage of accuracy?

Absolutely.

Most people can't handle that when they are beginners.

That's very true. That does come with experience in trading. You cannot be emotionally involved with a trade. You have to be willing to take a loss and even 12 losses in a row sometimes, while you are waiting for the big winners. A few big wins can offset quite a few losses.

What kind of methods do you use to get out of a trade?

We're supposed to reverse on new signals, but we do use some discretion.

What kind of stops do you use? Money management? Chart points?

The reversal stops are the trailing stops from the computer model. There is also a money management maximum. If that is closer than the computer model, we put it in until the model catches up. For example, in the S&P it's $2,500. In currencies it's $1,500; in soybeans $1,000; and so on.

It's a combination of a money management stop plus a system stop that's like a trailing stop that starts in the loss area.

Yes. You might call it a parabolic stop.

Kelly Angle

Kelly Angle is a money manager and author.

Kelly, how do you stand on cutting losses short?

You must cut losses short. This year I've introduced a totally new entry/exit strategy that I call *Cornucopia*. It uses $400 initial risk stops. When tested on four years of tick data, it produced the most consistent, most profitable results with the lowest loss figures of any system I've ever seen.

Most systems use market-generated stops. Most strategies using market-generated stops can't get you into the active markets for less than $1,000 to $3,000 per trade risk. The average individual simply can't afford that amount of risk. This is why a small money management stop is an absolute must.

What your system does to you when the markets aren't moving is more important than how your system performs during strong price trends. If you as a trader want to assess your system's ability to hold down losses, you might try this experiment. Examine your historical results and take out the double-digit up months. Then add the remaining single-digit up months and the down months. If the total is at least zero, or ideally, above zero, your system is giving you a risk-free environment in between major price moves.

You say that most systems require you to use fairly large stops. But you have a system that uses $400 stops in each market. What's different about your entry method that allows you to use such small stops?

For one, it doesn't care if we miss a major move.

It's more selective.

It doesn't overtrade, but it trades at about the same velocity as an average trend-following approach. It trades about twice a month per market. It waits for price compression to take place so you have a controlled environment in which to enter. Then you have more reliable conditions in which to place a smaller stop.

In other words, you don't enter if volatility is too great. You wait for relatively low volatility so that you can use a smaller stop safely.

Right.

Bob Jubb

Bob Jubb publishes newsletters on commodities, stocks, and options.

Bob, how important is cutting losses short in your approach?

After you filter your potential trades using the two-to-one reward to risk ratio, that is the key to it all. But cutting your losses short is involved in that. Over the past 20 years my method has only made about 24 trades a year on average. Trading that infrequently, too big a loss can really hurt you, especially if you're new to commodities and haven't made much money yet.

I'd say the average person starts with $10,000. If he should happen to trade with no stops, let one trade get carried away and lose $5,000, he's probably finished forever trading commodities. If you use my approach strictly, which is never to risk more than $1,000 a trade, you would have to be wrong 10 times in a row to wipe out your $10,000. You would have to be wrong five times in a row to drop to the 50 percent loss level where most people start to panic.

So cutting your losses short is the key to being around to participate in some big moves. For instance, take the $5,000 and $10,000 potential moves of a market like coffee. If you aren't controlling your losses, you won't be around to catch one of those. It's like being in a game where you need defense and offense. If you are unable to cut your losses, you're not playing any defense and you won't be around at the end to come from behind and win the game.

You mentioned that you never risk more than $1,000. Is that how you place your stop generally—to risk $1,000—or do you have other methods?

When I write my letter during the middle of the week, I recommend an entry at the market the next Monday. So I don't know exactly where the entry will be. I suggest risking $1,000. If the market moves in our favor, in the next letter I recommend a stop $1,000 from the current price. I may also vary it according to where support and resistance are.

It is generally $1,000, but it may vary depending on the market. For instance, in the Japanese yen I have found you need to risk $1,250, which is 100 points. On the other hand, I have hardly ever found it necessary to risk that much in corn or oats.

How much do you risk in corn and oats?

Usually $700 to $800. It depends on where I got in or where the current price is in relation to where a key chart point would be in danger.

Why don't you just use the key chart point?

Sometimes that would require risking $1,500. Over 20 years I've found that it's better to have certain rigid rules that you follow religiously. Otherwise, all of a sudden you'll end up believing in a market where you're actually wrong. That will eventually happen to all of us if we've been trading very long . . . like a week.

That is a simple approach.

I don't like complications. Over 20 years I've tried many fancy things and eventually thrown them all out. It's like quote machines. Three times I've paid to have quote machines installed in my office, and three times I've paid to have them removed.

I find I do much better in commodities when I just look at the newspaper the next day to see what happened. If something just falls apart on me, my stop takes me out.

What kind of accuracy have you had over time?

About 60 percent. There have been years where I have battled to make 45 percent and yet I have been profitable because you only need to catch two or three $5,000 trades to make your year.

If I bat 50 percent on 24 trades, that means I'll lose approximately $12,000 on my losing trades. If I catch two or three trades that make $5,000 and the other winners make only $1,000, I'd be up $10,000 for the year, which would be fine. I base everything on a $10,000 account. Many traders have $20,000 or $25,000, but I trade on the basis of a $10,000 account, which is fairly common.

ACCOUNT EQUITY STOPS

By account equity stops, I mean a stop based on a fixed percentage of your account equity. Like money management stops, these directly address the question of risk management and do not go at obvious places where other stops are lurking.

Nick Van Nice

Nick Van Nice is editor of Commodity Trend Service's various systems and hotlines.

Nick, what is your view on cutting losses short?

The first thing you need to do is determine what short is. I define all my stop-losses as a percentage of the account. I think it's very important to keep your losses around 2 percent of your overall equity. This will allow you to survive through a string of losses. You can lose even 10 times in a row and still have a drawdown of only 20 percent of your overall account.

Is that an outside limit for your stops or is that how you set your stops?

That's how I set the stops.

We understand you also prefer close-only stops. In other words, the market must close beyond the stop limit before you get out. Doesn't that increase your risk significantly?

Yes, I use strictly close-only stops. It does mean occasionally you get whacked pretty good. You'll take greater than a 2 percent loss, but that's the nature of the futures markets. It's very important to take the short-term noise out of the picture by using a close-only stop. They have been a big help to my trading.

Have you tested close-only stops versus regular stops?

Yes, and they come out better than just regular stops. Let me add this. In all the testing I've done, I found stops actually cut down the overall profitability of the systems we use here at Commodity Trend Service. In other words, the systems make more money without any stops at all.

You would rather have a reverse entry signal take you out of a position than a stop?

I won't say that. I'd rather have an exit signal take me out than a stop. But using a close-only stop seems to be the optimum way to trade.

Using an exit stop means you have a profitable position. What if you

don't have a profitable position? Then you've got to get a reverse signal, right?

Yes, but I'm also using the 2 percent rule. The first close below the 2 percent loss limit, and I'm getting out.

Do you always trade one contract using the 2 percent rule or do you have some method to use multiple contracts if 2 percent is a large amount?

No, I keep it simple. I only trade one contract.

What size of an account do you think is optimum for a 2 percent rule like that?

The 2 percent rule is something that you can use on all account sizes. The lower end of the range would be about $25,000. Anything smaller than $25,000 would not accommodate big enough stops using the 2 percent rule.

If you're going to take a $25,000 account and use a 2 percent stop, that's a $500 stop. You said you would only trade one contract. Does that mean you would use $4,000 stops in a $200,000 account?

No. I was thinking in terms of a $25,000 account. That's the size of our sample portfolios. We're comfortable with about a $500 loss per contract. So if you were trading a $100,000 account, you should trade four contracts.

Steve Briese

Steve Briese is editor of the *Bullish Review of Commodity Futures Markets* newsletter.

Steve, how important is cutting losses short to you?

Cutting losses short is certainly important to trading success. However, improperly done it will assure that you *won't* be successful. You won't profit. My idea of cutting losses short is that every trade must have a cutoff point. That cutoff point is the place you're stopped out of the trade because you know you're wrong.

I never base that cutoff point on a dollar loss. I always base it on where I know I am wrong on the trend that I am trading. If you cut your losses short simply on the basis of a dollar risk or percentage of your account, then you're not really following any kind of technical system.

As we have previously discussed, in order to be profitable, you must trade with the trend. You don't want to get out of a trade as long as the trend is going your way. Your stop-loss should be designed to get you out of the trade when you know the trend has changed and is now going against you. The key is to *adjust your entry point* so that your total risk on the trade will be a small portion of your capital, whether that's 1, 2, or 5 percent.

That's interesting. Let's say you have a trade where from the natural entry point, the risk is $1,000. Because of his account size, the trader wants to use a $500 stop. Some people might say if I'm not going to pass the trade because the risk is too large, I'm going to enter at the natural place and then adjust the protective stop closer to limit risk.

I never use a money management stop.

You would say that person would be getting out of his trade too soon because the correct stop was $500 further away. You prefer to adjust the entry to a point $500 from the correct stop. In effect, you would be getting in too early by anticipating or getting in too late by waiting for a reaction after the natural entry point. They are two different ways to attack the same problem, and you say your way is clearly correct and the other way is clearly wrong.

The first approach you described is a typical trading strategy that uses a money management stop. Trading books tell you where the stop should be for a particular price pattern. If that's risking too much money, then you are supposed to use a closer stop. But that assures you are no longer trading a pure system.

I have many new traders call me and want to ask about a specific trade. The first thing I ask them is where their stop-loss is going to be. They usually know where they want it. It should be the point on that chart where they know they're going to be wrong. Then I ask them how much money they want to risk. The response is, "I don't know."

I ask, "How much is in your account?" We arrive at a figure, and maybe because they have a small account, it's only $200. That's all they can afford to risk on the trade. What do I tell them to do?

I tell them to put their entry at the point they just figured for the stop-loss and to put a money management stop $200 below that entry. You know, more times than not those trades will work out.

You tell them to enter where they were going to get out?

That's right. The reason it works is they're no dummies. They've read all the books. They know where everybody else is getting out. They wanted to get out at the same point. The trouble is everybody is getting out at that point. That's just the time to get in.

Wouldn't you have a lot lower percentage accuracy in your trades if you adjust your entry so that it isn't at the correct entry point? Wouldn't that cut the percentage of time the market is going to keep moving after you get in?

That's why I use confirming tools. My favorite, of course, is the Commitments of Traders. I like to see some smart money coming into the market when the trend in the time frame I am trading is currently against me. That gives me an idea they are going to turn the trend around to the direction I want to go.

You can do similar things based on the longer-term trend. You can do it based on cycles. There are a lot of ways to do it. You want to find a reason why the market that you want to trade is about to reverse. For a lot of traders, when all things are considered, if they would start by calculating where their stop-loss should be, they would have a real knack for determining where they really ought to be entering.

That's fascinating. Let me see if I can summarize. You start with the concept that you only want to lose a certain amount of money per trade, and whether that's based on a percentage of your equity or your comfort level, that's where you start. Let's say somebody has a large account so the amount isn't all that crucial. Then you use a percentage of the account to set the loss amount. How much might that be?

I think 1 percent of your account is where you would like to be.

We'll assume 1 percent is the comfortable stop for our account. Then we look at a potential trade and see where our projected entry and our stop-loss will be. Our stop is going to be the point where the trend will have turned against us.

- We calculate how much we're going to lose if we're stopped out. If that's within the 1 percent tolerance, then we can take the trade as is. Depending on how small the loss is, we might be able to trade multiple contracts and still keep our loss to within 1 percent.

- However, if the loss is not within the 1 percent tolerance, we must adjust our *entry point* to bring it close enough to the exit point so our risk is no more than 1 percent.

- After we adjust the entry point, we look to see if we can find some confirming indications that the trade will move from our adjusted entry point to the more preferable entry point we first selected before it turns around and hits our stop. Is that the idea?

That describes it.

The other idea you had was to consider entering at your exit point and putting your stop somewhat away from that.

Let's assume we're going to take a long position. Most people can figure out pretty well where the stop-loss should be. Their account size dictates that they must buy somewhere between that point and the optimal entry point. They must wait for additional weakness where price approaches their stop point. But where do you buy on weakness? There is no good way to determine how much weakness to wait for. Using the stop-loss point as the entry point is a pretty good short-cut method.

MARGIN-BASED STOPS

By margin-based stops, I mean a stop calculated by taking a percentage of the exchange margin for the commodity you are trading. The rationale is that margin represents a measure of volatility and risk. Another way to express the same approach is in terms of a multiple or percentage of a limit move in the market (if it has limits—not all markets do).

Colin Alexander

Colin Alexander is editor of *The Wellspring Futures Newsletter.*

How do you cut your losses short?

I use a combination of half a limit move, chart points, trendline crossings, and weekly reversals.

What's your definition of a weekly reversal?

In a bull market when price exceeds the preceding week's high and then closes the week at a point below the preceding week's close. And vice versa for a weekly reversal in a bear market.

I understand you are ambivalent about using stop-loss orders.

Of course, you should cut losses and not get married to a position. When I was a retail broker, I had somebody ride lumber down from 195 to 120 because he just couldn't believe the downtrend wasn't coming to an end.

There has to be a sensible tradeoff between cutting losses and giving a trade room to move. Anything too close is an invitation to give the market money for nothing. All you end up doing is taking an unnecessary loss where, strictly speaking, a retracement should be a place to put on more positions, not to be stopped out.

You don't find that half a limit move is too small?

That's a ballpark figure. I seldom want to take more than a 50-point loss in soybean oil or 50 cents in crude oil or 50 points in the Canadian dollar.

How did you reach these conclusions? Is it on the basis of testing or experience or what?

Experience.

How long have you been trading?

Fourteen years.

ECLECTIC METHODS
Jack Schwager

Jack Schwager is Director of Futures Research and Trading Strategy at Prudential Securities, Inc. He suggests different stop placement methods for different styles of trading.

How important is cutting losses short?

It is essential for the simplistic reason that if you don't do it, you literally have to be wrong only once to be out of the game. You only have to make one drastic mistake or be stubborn one time. If you were very bullish on bonds and stayed bullish over the last few months, you could have lost your entire account. Take any sustained trend, and if you are positioned the wrong way, it will be a disaster. So you must have some way of cutting losses.

Specifically, how do you approach the concept of cutting losses short?

The easiest advice I could give anybody is just to decide where you're getting out before you get in. But for those who can't trust themselves, put in a good-til-canceled liquidation order at the same time as you put in your entry order. Then you don't have to worry about it.

If you're a system trader, you have to build rules within your system that will keep you from being on the wrong side of any sustained market move. You also have to consider things such as leverage. Keep leverage to a point where you're not risking too much relative to what you're willing to risk or should risk.

What's a good guideline?

You can do it on a trade-by-trade basis. That's probably the most straightforward way. The commonly cited percentages tend to be 1 or 2 or a maximum of 3 percent of the account equity. For many people that is going to be difficult because their accounts are not large enough. That may be the same as saying you can't trade if you have a tiny account. Ideally, if you do it on a trade-by-trade basis, I would say 2 percent or lower on any given trade would be optimum. Probably 3 percent would be the maximum.

In terms of how you actually place your stop, what methods do you prefer?

There is a split here between subjective trading versus computerized trading. In the latter case—computerized trading—I don't believe in using stops. I just have rules that get me out of trades if the market goes significantly against me.

In terms of individual trades where you're making decisions using judgment, you should ask yourself, "Where might the market go so that I would no longer want to be in the trade?" Or, stated another way, "If I'm right, what should *not* happen?" The answer to that would be the stop point.

Alternatively, it might just be the amount that you are willing to risk on the trade. That point would not be technically significant because in many cases a technically significant stop may imply a loss that far exceeds a reasonable loss for your account.

You wouldn't have any theoretical problem with somebody who saw a trade they wanted to do, decided that an intelligent chart point was bigger than they should really risk, and then just went ahead and risked a smaller amount with which they felt comfortable in terms of risk management for their account size?

I wouldn't. But in order to do that, they should have some feeling that the timing is now. There should be something telling them to do the trade right now.

For system trading, do you just wait for your system to reverse?

I manage money using computerized methodologies. While there are literally hundreds of inputs that go into the strategy, not a single one of those is a stop condition. There are no stops. I have a distaste for stop orders when you're trading size. I don't know for sure that if you have sizable stop orders in the market, it will make it more likely for the market to hit that point, but it certainly can't help. There's no reason for showing your hand.

So I structured my approach to avoid the use of stops and achieve risk control in a different way. Those ways of achieving risk control include the following: diversify across an extraordinarily wide range of strategies and make sure those strategies include highly uncorrelated systems so it's very unlikely you'll have extremely large positions. I also diversify across as wide a range of markets as possible. In the broadest portfolio, I am trading over 50 markets. If you put all that together, you find you do not get extraordinarily wide equity swings against you.

For perspective, what's the minimum account size necessary to trade that kind of a system?

One million dollars. Literally, I designed this approach to trade one million dollars. You need that much to take advantage of being able to vary the position size of each trade. To me that's very important. I couldn't achieve what I consider satisfactory return to risk without the ability to vary the bet size.

I hope my friends have stimulated some thoughts for your own stop placement tactics. In the next chapter, we'll examine the concept of letting profits run, perhaps the hardest principle to follow of all.

CHAPTER 4

Let Profits Run

Over the years I have been struck by the consistency with which successful traders name exiting profitable trades as being the most difficult of the various trading decisions. Most aspiring traders spend almost all their time working on entry methods. This is probably because they believe that near-perfect entries can compensate for deficiencies in other areas. Since near-perfect entries are possible only in hindsight, experienced traders come around to the point where they place the least emphasis on entry.

The experts I interviewed had numerous ways of letting profits run. They can be roughly separated into the following categories: trailing stops, profit targets, and reverse system signals. Of those using trailing stops, they divided into methods based on indicators, volatility, chart patterns, and dollar amounts. Some said letting profits run was not important to them. Others used multiple methods.

TRAILING STOPS USING INDICATORS

Nick Van Nice

Nick Van Nice is editor of Commodity Trend Service's various systems and hotlines. He emphasizes long-term trading.

Nick, how important is letting profits run?

It's very important to let your profits run. One incidental benefit is that staying in a trade prevents you from taking additional signals from your system. It's vital to limit the number of trades your system makes. When you are trading long-term and in a winning position, it reduces risk by limiting additional trading.

In other words, when you are letting profits run, you're not allowing any pyramiding.

Exactly. There is generally not a lot of trending action to trade. When you finally do find a trend in a market where you are trading your system, it's important to be patient and let that trade work.

Is that another way of saying that your risk on leaving your position alone is less than the risk of trying to take a new position if you are shaken out of this one prematurely?

Right. This is especially true when you're using the 2 percent stop-loss rule that our system uses [keeping initial risk to 2 percent of account equity].

Are there other good reasons to let profits run?

Yes. The most important reason is that because of how difficult futures trading is, your key offensive weapon is the few great big moves you see in a year. Once you exit a market that's making a big move, it's so difficult to get back on board. Psychologically, emotionally, and financially, it's very hard to reenter a move that you've already exited. That's *my* biggest difficulty anyway.

You get into a trade and it shows you $7,000 or $8,000. It's exceeded your expectations and hits your profit target. You get out, but it turns out the thing is just getting started. If you are a trend follower, it's the few huge trades each year that make your bottom line. If you're trying to slug it out with short-term trading, you're going to lose more than you win because of the costs of trading. They add up quickly for short-term traders. It's simple arithmetic. Your winners have to be big. To get them, you must let your winning trades develop as long as possible.

How do you let your profits run?

There are two ways: either you use a trailing stop or you don't. I have systems that don't have a trailing stop, and I like that method of trading. You let your system's indicators take you out when it's time to take profits by generating an entry in the opposite direction.

The other way is to use a very long-term moving average to trail a stop. I like a 45–50 day moving average, and I like using a close-only stop.

A somewhat subtle distinction is using a different exit method for profitable and losing positions. When a position becomes profitable, it's often best to use longer-term indicators with that profitable position than you do with a losing position. That's one key secret of our *Trendsetter System*. We use much longer-term and more stringent requirements to get out of a profitable position than we do a losing position. To take it a step further, you may want to consider using a close-only stop on your winning positions while using a normal protective stop on new positions.

When you say your indicators, you can't be referring to a reverse entry signal because that would require you to wait nine months for an opposite trend to be established.

Right.

So it's more like a very long-term trailing stop, in effect.

You move it along every day. There are three very long-term moving averages and two shorter-term indicators. All of them have to turn for us to have an exit signal.

That's a different kind of exit signal than your entry signal though. Is that what you're saying?

Yes.

But you also have an alternative of just a long-term moving average.

That's right.

How do you decide between the two?

Whichever occurs first.

Colin Alexander

Colin Alexander is editor of *The Wellspring Futures Newsletter.*

Colin, how important as a principle is letting profits run?

Extremely important. There's absolutely no question that if you don't bank some really big trades, you'll never pay for the harassment and nickel and diming to death on the ones that don't work. Even under optimum circumstances, you are not going to achieve more than about a 50 percent winning percentage.

Once a trade starts to move and I have a profit, I'm prepared to give it in round numbers a full limit move to one-and-a-half times a limit move in which to react. For example, in cotton I might give the market as much as 200 or 300 points if the trend was strong and I had a profit cushion to work with.

It sounds like you're using some kind of a trailing stop with your winning trades.

Yes, using chart points. I watch for weekly reversals and persistent adverse daily chart action.

It sounds very subjective.

Yes, it is. In my experience, conditions for different markets are seldom amenable to absolute rules. The way you might expect the Canadian dollar to act is quite different from the way pork bellies might behave.

Before someone else can trade with that amount of subjectivity, how many years of experience do you think they need?

Somebody should be able to get a handle on it within about a year.

What other indicators do you watch?

It's a little bit like flying a Boeing 747. You can't only work with the altimeter and the gyro compass. I pay attention to perhaps 10 or 12 prime indicators.

Jack Schwager

Jack Schwager is director of futures research and trading strategy at Prudential Securities, Inc. He is also a coprincipal of Wizard Trading, a commodity money management firm.

Jack, how important is letting profits run?

For a trend-oriented trader it's essential. In Edwin LeFevre's book, *Reminiscences of a Stock Operator*, a fictionalized treatment of Jesse Livermore, he says, "It was never my thinking that made the big money for me. It was always my sitting." That's a very apt comment. It means that you don't have to be a genius, you don't have to be smarter than anybody else, but you do need the patience to stay with a correct position. When you are positioned in a major trade, you want to be able to exploit at least a substantial chunk of the move. That is critical.

It's a matter of style. My style is to take a few of those exceptional moves and be able to break even everywhere else.

How do you go about letting your profits run? Do you use trailing stops?

Letting profits run is pretty easy to do and pretty easy to explain. Essentially, if you use a long-term crossover moving average system and follow it, you will necessarily let your profits run. It will raise other problems, but I use it as an illustration of a potential answer to your question. Just off the top of my head, let's say you use a 125-day crossover moving average on some market; when you get a major move, you will indeed ride it for the long term. You will capture it. It's easy to see how it can be done.

The thing with letting your profits run in practice is that you don't necessarily know ahead of time which will be the true major moves and which will be the ones that go part way and then come back. For instance, a 125-day crossover moving average will kill you if you're trading currency markets like we've had over the last year and a half. In my mind, no single strategy will do it. You have to combine different strategies.

Michael Chisholm

Michael Chisholm is editor of the *Taurus* advisory service, now in its 20th year of publication.

Michael, how important is letting profits run?

In our previous discussion about these principles I used an automobile analogy. Your four key principles are like the four tires on a car. If any of them are flat, your trading will have a very bumpy ride. If too many blow out, you won't go anywhere.

How do you handle the process of letting profits run?

To me trailing stops are an absolute must. I typically lock my profits in by trailing stops of one sort or another. It depends upon the length of trading involved—short term or long term. My personal trading is in the 30- to 60-day time frame.

I prefer a mechanical method of moving stops as opposed to using judgment. My preferred methods use moving averages and channels. I found that even though they may be simplistic compared to some of the more exotic kinds of indicators out there, they work best. I'm a believer that sometimes the simplest things work best.

I also believe it's necessary to have a method of reentry with the trend in case the market hits your trailing stop prematurely. Sometimes it's the original entry methodology, but typically I will reenter more quickly than I would enter a brand new trade. I might enter on the open the next day after a signal instead of waiting for further confirmation like I do on an initial entry.

I've tried using profit targets. I went through a period for a couple of years where I tried every type of profit target imaginable. I was unable to come up with a methodology that worked as consistently and profitably as trailing stops. I prefer them by far.

Profit targets are unrealistic. Markets gain momentum, whether upward or downward. They have a tendency to take on a life of their own. They just keep running. As a result, I've never been able to use profit targets effectively.

The reason I prefer a mechanical methodology is because greed and fear enter the picture maybe more so here than anywhere else in trading. We always want to squeeze more out of a trade, and at the same time we're afraid we're going to lose some or all of our profits. I'm much better off having a mechanical way of exiting profitable trades.

When you do your testing, do you use the same rules and the same parameters for each market or do you customize them?

It's tempting to customize because you can get some dynamite results. But most people agree that would be overoptimization. I insist on using the same variables for all commodities.

As I recall, you don't move your initial stop until your trailing stop indicator is at least at the breakeven point. Is that correct?

Yes. For a long time I thought breakeven stops were valuable. As I've done more testing over the years, I've come to the conclusion that breakeven stops don't serve any real function other than psychological comfort.

I don't necessarily use the same indicator for my trailing stop as I do for the initial stop. For instance, I may use a 30-day moving average for my initial protective stop. Then I may use something entirely different like an 11-day channel or an 18-day moving average for the trailing stop. But I never start using the trailing stop until it's at least at the breakeven point or better.

Then you follow it every day and move it closer to the trade but not farther away?

Yes, as long as it's within limit range. If it's out of limit range, I might let it sit for a few days.

As a practical matter.

Right.

But in terms of the system, theoretically you could move it every day.

Yes.

Do you keep the same trailing stop method throughout the trade or do you change your trailing stop method depending on how profitable the trade becomes?

Right now I use the same trailing stop method no matter how much profit is in the trade. I went through a period of time where if the RSI (Wilder's Relative Strength Index) reached a certain overbought level or a certain oversold level, I would tighten the trailing stop. With more computer testing, I found that didn't work as well as using the same trailing stop rule throughout the trade.

You mentioned using less rigorous rules to reenter after your trailing stop took you out of a trade. Doesn't that reduce the effectiveness of the trailing stop? If you're going to get right back in, aren't you wasting your time to exit in the first place?

That's a fine line. Sometimes that is the case. At other times I've seen the trailing stop take me out on a correction while my key indicators all remained in alignment.

I can see a reentry method that, for instance, on a long trade gets you back in if the market makes a new high. But to get right back in on the next day's open seems like a waste of a commission.

I reenter only if the indicators are still in alignment. Sometimes it works well, and other times it doesn't. Ninety percent of the time when my trailing stop is hit, one of the entry indicators has shifted and I'm not going to reenter.

TRAILING STOPS

Kelly Angle

Kelly Angle formerly published *The Timing Device* advisory service, but since this interview he has become a full-time money manager.

Kelly, let's talk about letting profits run.

Trends in the markets today are different than 5 to 10 years ago. Now, most of the time prices move vertically because a large trader is exiting a position and creating a false breakout. For example, let's say a manager is in a currency. The market is quiet, and he dumps his short position. Prices rally for a day and a half while other traders respond to the upmove. It generates a $1,000 to $1,500 move per contract. There is no additional buying to sustain the move so prices fall back to where they were originally.

Unless a trader who gets triggered into these types of false breakouts (or mini-trends if you want to call them that) can handle and take advantage of them, he's not going to survive long enough to see the really major price moves that extend over a period of weeks or months.

I believe in a flexible approach to taking profits that can adapt to short- and long-term price movement. In my approach I can take a profit in a few hours or hold on to a major move for weeks. By having this flexibility, you can produce accuracy numbers that are close to 50 percent. That is a more palatable trading style from an emotional point of view.

The obvious major league question is how do you take profits quickly without missing the big moves? How do you know when you're going to have a big move and when you're not?

It depends entirely upon your trade position. It doesn't matter what the market is doing or is going to do. Your risk element is totally dependent upon your particular trade location. I got to thinking about this because in Jack Schwager's first *Wizards* book, Paul Tudor Jones talked about how he looked at each trade as if he had put it on yesterday. To me what that meant was that when you put a trade on, your biggest risk is in the first few hours or the first few days.

When you're using a small stop like I do, if you're wrong, you're gone. I've lost trades within five minutes. Generally, if I'm wrong, I'm out in the first day or two. If you get profits within the first few hours, then this might be one of those phenomena where a major trader is exiting a position and you'll have a little day-and-a-half rally or a day-and-a-half selloff. Markets tend to move in one- to three-day increments.

There has been a fad lately for traders to try and capture that one- to three-day phenomenon. I bought systems examining it. I looked at it and tested it. I concluded that for me it's a ridiculous time frame. All the work I've done prior to this told me that if you default to taking those small profits, you ruin your capacity to hold on to an extended move. Economically in this business, the minute you deprive yourself of the extended trade, you have a difficult time making long-term profits.

In other words, if you take a profit at a $1,000 price objective, you eliminate your capacity to have a $5,000 to $10,000 move. In the trading style I've been pursuing over the last 10 years, you were better off holding out for the major moves. Over the long haul, your survival is dependent upon your ability to make the large trade.

But while you're waiting, you see all these small trades come and go. You ask yourself why you let that $1,000 move go by. Is there an alternative theory? Yes.

The alternative theory is this. I call it the Blood Flow Theory. Let's say your system makes 100 percent over the year. However, in the first 10 months, it had a 50 percent drawdown while it was waiting for some of those big trades. Most people won't get to the last two months. The drawdown would have drained their body of 50 percent of their blood, and they would have been too weak to carry on.

These small-trade opportunities appear pretty regularly. At the very minimum you can reduce your risk to zero. If you can capitalize on a small profit, then do it. If a market rallies for a $1,000 profit in a day and a half, a person should be very aggressive in moving their exit stop at least to breakeven if not higher.

What happens then is a function of how well new buying or new selling comes in to drive prices farther. If that happens, the market is telling you that new participants are feeding the trend. That is a sign you should stop being aggressive in tightening your stop. If a trade continues to be profitable, I gradually move the stop away from the market. That gives me the potential to hold the trade through some subsequent noise that will always occur over the life of a one- to five-week trade.

As I understand it, you prefer the long-term move if you can get it, but you realize that you can still make a lot of money with the short-term moves. So you're not totally opposed to taking a quick profit if it's there. The way you do it is by using a very aggressive trailing stop during the first few days. If it makes you take profits right away, that's fine. If your trade lasts longer than a few days, even with your aggressive stop, now you think that this shows the potential for a longer-term move. So you back off your trailing stop and go into long-term mode. Is that right?

Yes. The key to this is not so much that you can make a lot of money from short-term trades, but in the majority of cases, you're reducing your risk exposure by taking a small profit of $300 to $600 within the first few hours or the first day or two. That goes a long way toward paying for the opportunity cost you're risking per trade (the initial stop size). It's really to help smooth out your equity curve.

When you start holding positions for long-term moves, you might have 50 percent of your total account in open equity. Your closed equity may be taking serious hits even though your total equity is up. Taking some smaller profits every so often replenishes your closed equity and makes it more consistent over time.

From my testing I've found that the tighter stops replenish the closed equity balance more consistently and improve the percentage accuracy closer to 50 percent. Those are two good things, both for your account and for your state of mind.

Do you have a reentry strategy if you're stopped out with these aggressive tactics?

Yes, if the market doesn't become too volatile.

But sometimes you're going to miss the big move because you got out too quick.

Yes. Here's another thing, though. When you test your system, you'll find that even if the market went on and made a big move, your system may still end up exiting very near that short-term profit point near the beginning of the trade. You will always leave some of the potential profit on the table, so taking a nice short-term profit may not penalize you as much as you might think.

When you look at the open profit generated in most long-term approaches and compare that to how much they actually closed out, the percentage is quite low. People would be staggered to see what the total maximum open profit generated by a long-term system is. It's generally huge, and even great systems actually take out only about one-fifth of that total potential.

Walter Bressert

Walter Bressert is a cycle trader who likes to trade multiple contract positions.

Walt, how important is letting profits run to trading success?

For many people the most money they've made in the market has come when they managed to hold on to something for a long period of time. Early in my trading career I found that the really big money is made in the big moves. But the problem always was how do you hold on to the big moves. How do you do that and maintain your sanity?

To hold on for a big move, you're going to have to give back 25 to 35 percent of your profits at least once in that move. For most people that's an intolerable amount. They can't take the pain.

Before you make the decision to let your profits run, you must devise a strategy that will allow you comfortably to let the market move against you without destroying your equilibrium. Once you've lost your equilibrium, then no matter what you do, you're not going to trade properly. I guess the next question is, How do you do it?

Yes.

I start with the basic trend, which takes me back to my primary cycle. If I have called the primary (weekly) cycle bottom correctly, the market will go up afterwards for a minumum number of weeks. If the next longer cycle, the seasonal cycle, is moving up, then the weekly cycle is going to have what I call right translation. It is going to go up for a longer period of time than it goes down. I can look forward to a market that will be generally rising for at least six weeks, sometimes two or three months.

Based on the previous performance of cycles of the same length, I set up an expectation as to what price and time objectives I should see. These levels would have occurred in about 70 percent of the other cycles. Once I have my time and price objectives, I have a goal. Until I reach that goal, I'm generally not concerned that the market will go too far the other way. I'm comfortable with letting it move against me.

The second part of the strategy is how do you exit the position if you're wrong and the market does not reach your goal. I use three different trailing stops to tell me if I'm wrong. These include price patterns that generate opposite direction entry signals to tell me that my position is wrong, at least temporarily.

I break my trading up into three different time frames: a short-term, an intermediate-term, and a long-term time period. I pick a trailing stop for each.

For my long-term time frame, the stop is a long way from the market. It's far enough away that if the market has a minor correction, it will not affect my position. But it will also get me out of a bad trade without costing me a great deal of money.

If you have three different trailing stops, isn't the shorter one always going to be hit first?

When I first enter a position all three time frames have the same stop. Once the market has moved away from my entry, I usually take profits on the shortest time frame position within five market days from the time I get in. Once I take off my first position, I start to move my stop up for the second one. When I exit the second one, I move my stop up on the third.

So you trade three positions.

Three to five. But let's say three to keep it simple: short term, intermediate term, and long term.

You trade three separate contracts or groups of contracts, and you have three trailing stops. They will get you out of your three positions at different times and different prices.

I look at the market from a short-term perspective to get in. The short-term time frame tells me price is likely to rise up to a particular level. That's where I should be taking my short-term profit.

If I change my time frame at that point to a longer-term one, the trade could be looking really good. Just where I would be taking a profit, I might also be thinking about holding the position for the long term. If I kept my short-term position, the market might turn around and nail me and I wouldn't make anything. By using three separate positions in three separate time frames, profits on the first two give me a cushion to take advantage of the big move in the third.

In effect, it's like using three different systems at the same time.

Yes. It is one entry with three different ways to lock in profits.

Robert Miner

Robert Miner is a Gann trader and Editor of the *Major Market Analysis Report.*

Bob, how important is letting profits run?

I'm not sure what the percentages are, but it's a small percentage of your trades that generates the vast majority of profits. You have to remain in a trade to capture the market's potential to have a strong swing.

How do you stay with your trades?

At each point the market confirms I'm correct, I move the stop a bit closer. I call them trending continuations.

Based on what?

Everything is based on time, price, and pattern. If you're right, all three should be telling you the same thing. Pattern has a good deal to do with it, but it also has to do with price levels. Once price exceeds a certain level, more than likely it's going to run to the next level. If price takes out a level and immediately flips back, it's like a false breakout, which is one of the clearest signals that you're wrong.

At the same time, you're also looking for signals in the other direction. If you see a conjunction of price and time going the other way while you have a profitable position on, do you want to take the reverse signal or do you want to stay with a good profitable position?

The vast majority of times I just bring my trailing stop really close. I let the market tell me. If it's a strong coincidence of projections, I might bring the stop all the way up to the previous day's low (for long positions). Or if it simply closes below the opening, then there could be a reversal if there's any sign of weakness.

TRAILING STOPS BASED ON VOLATILITY

Russell Wasendorf

Russell Wasendorf is editor of *Futures Factors.*

Russ, how do you look at this principle?

Letting profits run relates very much to trend analysis. One of the things I simply do not do is get out of a position just because it has moved in a major way for me on that particular day. I'd rather let the market take me out of the position by hitting my stop.

You would definitely be opposed to the idea of some kind of short-term, quick-profit-taking methods?

Absolutely. If you are establishing your stops based on the volatility of the market, hopefully the volatility will not take you out until the trend is changing or is about to change. Increased volatility usually occurs at major tops in the market. Therefore, you let the market run to its peak and at the last moment, you give up a little bit at the top.

So you're using a trailing stop based on volatility.

Right.

What time period do you use to measure volatility?

It is a 30-day weighted moving average where recent volatility is the most important. I recalculate the stop on a daily basis.

You haven't said anything about how important letting your profits run is to overall profitability.

You have structured this interview in a very interesting way. On a scale of one to three, number one is following the trend. Number two is protecting the position with stops or cutting losses short. The third, in my opinion, is letting profits run.

TRAILING STOPS BASED ON CHART PATTERNS

Bill Gary

Bill Gary is editor of the CIS *Price Perceptions* newsletter. It was the top performing advisory service followed by *Commodity Traders Consumer Report* during the difficult year of 1993.

Bill, how do you treat the concept of letting profits run?

Letting profits run is as important as cutting losses short because you never know exactly what's going to happen tomorrow. It can rain in Brazil or something else unexpected can happen. The odd thing is that events tend to follow the market. In other words, if we're in a good uptrend in a market, you'll find that the news events will tend to follow that trend. If you've left the market just because you made a good profit and there is a surprise news event, you may leave an awful lot on the table. At the end of the year the extra profits you make by letting your profits run will normally make the difference in whether you have a profit or a loss in your trading account. So it's critically important to let your profits run.

How do you do that?

I use trailing stops. After I've established a base position and the market begins to perform, I will move my stop up gradually below major support areas or below a Fibonacci pullback or something of that nature.

It's a chart-based trailing stop?

Yes. Then as we get into the latter stages of the move, I change tactics. I look at the last, largest pullback that we've had in the market and use that distance as my trailing stop. For instance, assume we're long sugar and the last break was 60 points, after which it turned around and went into new high ground. If we're in the latter stages of the move, I use that 60-point break to determine my trailing stop. I set it at 62 or 65 points below the current price. I let the market go as far as it will. Eventually it will turn around and stop me out. I don't try to pick a top.

If you have another smaller reaction and you're still in the trade, would you make the trailing stop smaller in line with the latest reaction?

Yes. Let's say we had a 60-point setback and then the market moved into new high ground and then it came back and fell quickly 35 points before turning around to make another new high. I would change my trailing stop to 35 points plus a few points. I'd continue to tighten it like that until I am eventually stopped out.

How do you define what a major setback is? What's the difference between a major setback that you consider and a minor setback that you ignore?

Normally it is an Elliott Wave move. I watch the Elliott Wave from a very basic viewpoint, but I do watch it closely. Bull markets tend to go up in three primary legs and have two setbacks. Conversely, bear markets do the same thing. They have three down legs with two corrections. When we're in the third leg of a move, then we know we're in the latter stages, but we have no idea as to where it's going to extend. I use the Elliott Wave retracements to tell me what kind of trailing stop I should use. Normally, I would not have a stop tighter than about a 40 percent retracement of the most recent upleg. I always allow the market at least a 38 percent retracement.

In other words, if I were long sugar and it went to 12 cents and dropped back to 11.40, then went higher to 12.20 and dropped back to 11.80, we would be in the third leg when it made a new high after that. After the first leg, I would use a 60-point-plus trailing stop. After the reaction back to 11.90, as long as that reaction to 11.90 is not less than 38 percent of the most recent advance (which would be from 11.40 to 12.20), I would use the 40-point reaction to set the new trailing stop. In the example, the last reaction is 50 percent of the previous upleg, so I would use it to advance my trailing stop.

Glen Ring

Glen Ring is editor of the *Trends in Futures* newsletter.

Glen, how do you feel about letting profits run?

That feeds back into cutting losses short. It's having a plan on how you're going to manage a trade once you get into it. You must have a way to manage your position. I try to trade with the trend. If I catch a trending move, I must have a way to maximize that opportunity to cover all my small losses.

I constantly receive phone calls from people who are in the market but have no idea how to proceed. I ask them how they are going to manage the trade: What was your plan? They say they really didn't have one.

It's the planning and the preparation that count. The game is won before you get into the market—not on any given trade but on the overall approach. Planning is so important. The vast majority of people have no idea how they're going to let profits run. When they do get into a big trade, they're just like a dog chasing a car. When they catch it, they don't know what to do with it. They're bewildered and lost.

When I'm teaching seminars, I use an example of a trade I made a couple of years ago in feeder cattle. I bought the market. I fully expected to make $800 on the trade, but by having a plan to make the market take me out and let profits run, I ended up netting something close to $3,500 when I was expecting to make $800. If I didn't have a plan on how to manage it, I may have blindly taken profits at $800. How many losing trades will one big winner like that offset?

How do you let profits run?

If I'm trading a trending pattern where a market is making higher highs and higher lows or lower highs and lower lows, for the most part I bring the stop to just below the previous reaction low or just above the previous reaction high.

How do you define a reaction?

A reaction has to run three days or more to qualify. Occasionally, we have markets that stretch out so far they don't give you a reaction. All of a sudden your trade is four or five limits into the money. I call those extraordinary markets, and I take extraordinary means to protect my profits. When I'm trading for myself, I'll usually reduce my position size.

If you have a market that truly takes on a parabolic form, reactions may shorten to as little as a day. The market breaks for a day or two and moves back to new highs. Once a market goes parabolic, that defines a reaction for me.

The main thing I do is follow the reaction lows and highs with trailing stops. It's a simple process. People could do it with a moving average if they want to. If they want to protect a percentage of equity, they can do it that way. If they want to use a volatility band, they can do it that way.

TRAILING STOPS USING DOLLAR AMOUNTS

Bob Jubb

Bob Jubb is editor of *Tomorrow's Commodities*, one of the few advisory services that operates without a hotline.

Bob, how important is letting profits run?

It's important, but not as important as your other three principles. If you can get two or three good moves a year, it's because you let your profits run.

As I indicated in our previous discussion, I start a trade with a $1,000 money management stop. I try to find a logical chart point in that vicinity. The first time I consider moving my stop is when I have a $2,000 profit. At $3,000 I usually risk at least $1,500, and at $4,000 I'm out 99 percent of the time risking half of it. In other words, I always try to let half my profit go before abandoning the trade. The only time I narrow my trailing stop back to a $500 risk is when the seasonals are going against me or the chart is showing some sign of topping out.

This is where my 20 years of experience come in. There are some markets I trust more than others. If things look like they're starting to go wrong, especially if it took a few months to get the $2,000 profit, I might move the stop up more aggressively. If it took only a few weeks, I wouldn't want to miss what might be an exciting trend.

The longer it takes to achieve the profit, the more likely I'm going to tighten up and protect more of it. Traditionally I let 50 percent be exposed. If I'm up $6,000, I'm going to have the stop probably $3,000 above where I entered. I'll leave the other $3,000 exposed so I can try to ride the trend to wherever it's going. This is especially true if you're in something like coffee that periodically has a $10,000 to $15,000 run. You wouldn't want to worry about $3,000 when you might still have $9,000 on the table.

When you're calculating how much open profit you have on a trade, do you use the most favorable extreme or the most favorable close?

The close.

Do you use close-only stops or regular stops?

Regular stops.

Let's say you have a big move and you've got $10,000 in profits. You're moving your stop up to protect $5,000. That's a lot to leave on the table. You're not locked into that if the market starts to look like it's making a top, are you?

If I were up $10,000 and had been looking for $12,000 at the most, I might tighten my stop to risk $1,000 because I see only $2,000 more in potential reward.

So another way to consider your trailing stop would be to reassess the risk/reward ratio and move your trailing stop up to protect half what you think the remaining reward might be?

Yes. I don't try to be cute and pick the top. I'm just looking for the middle of the move. By using trailing stops, you can get a good piece of the moves that you're in. I've probably never captured 90 percent of a move. To do that you're going to have to pretty much pick the bottom and pick the top. I don't even attempt to do that.

You don't have to pick tops and bottoms to do quite well, do you? Especially if you have the discipline to let profits run.

If you don't trade too often and if you can get two or three big profits during the year while limiting all your losses to roughly $1,000, you'll almost assuredly have a profitable year.

There's some luck involved in being in the right markets, isn't there?

Absolutely. I found myself in coffee one day not knowing how I got there, and I made about $7,900.

There's a certain amount of luck, but over time the luck is eliminated. In the short term (like a year) there is luck involved.

Yes. If the first thing you ever did was buy a coffee contract in the middle of a trend and you made 12 grand, you could start to think you knew what you were doing. Over the years, I've learned the markets will teach you it's not that easy.

Do you have any other ideas on letting profits run?

Sometimes when I move a stop on a profitable position, I look at the previous week's low and go 30 or 40 points under it. Also, I always try to place a stop under an even number. In that regard, if I'm going below 19.00, I don't place the stop at 18.90. I'll go down to 18.80 or 18.75. When I talk to floor traders, they say there are so many stops at 18.90 that when the market goes below 19.00, it going to go at least down to 18.90 just to get those stops. I always try to avoid the obvious places where most people would put their stops. That means I usually go 20 ticks over or under the even numbers. This applies to trailing stops on profitable positions, not initial stops where I'm more concerned about limiting the loss.

PROFIT TARGETS
Peter Brandt

Peter Brandt is a long-time professional trader and editor of *The Factor* newsletter. He specializes in trading classical chart patterns.

Peter, how do you react to the principle of letting profits run?

Every trade I put on has a predetermined profit target at which I most likely will liquidate a trade. In this sense I do not believe in letting profits run. It's a matter of how you define your terms. Letting profits run would be an approach where one does not have a profit target in mind but rather allows the market to keep moving by some mechanism of moving stops until the market reverses against the position. In that sense I do not let profits run.

When I enter a trade, I have a predetermined stop-loss point and a predetermined target. If the market reaches that target, more often than not I come out of the trade.

I am not a believer in automatically trailing stops by some dollar amount. As a trade develops and moves towards my target, I keep my initial protective stop. Eventually, this causes my risk/reward relationship to get way out of whack. As the market approaches my profit target, I have a smaller and smaller additional potential profit, but a larger and larger loss if the market retraces to my stop point. This has been a source of consternation over the years.

Your protective stop is far away and your target's fairly close?

Yes. All of a sudden I come to a point where the market is $200 from where I want to get out, but I still have my stop $1,400 away. That's a problem area of my trading. When I start developing a large degree of discomfort with a particular trade in those cases, I start looking at charts to find excuses to move my stop up.

So you do trail stops sometimes?

Yes, but I don't like to do it on a dollar basis. I'd rather do it with chart points, such as recent minor reactions.

You don't have an automatic way of doing it. You use judgment?

Right.

Are your target points chart pattern targets?

Yes. They're measurements based on the charts. I describe how to determine chart pattern targets in my book *Trading Commodity Futures with Classical Chart Patterns.*

One of the things that you're not able to do if you take profits at

targets is capture the really big moves. Many successful traders say
that's where the big money is made—on the big moves. Your chart
pattern targets are usually not that far away. How do you react to that?

I have two answers. First, if you're basing your target on weekly or monthly
charts, you can develop some substantial targets. For instance, cotton recently
made a measured move of $6,000 a contract. That is not a small profit.

How do you decide whether to use the target from the daily, weekly,
or monthly chart if they all have a pattern?

If there's a clear monthly or weekly chart pattern, I will use that. The
second part of my answer to your previous question is that while I may not
take $10,000 profits using my approach, at the same time, I don't take $2,000
losses. There's a tradeoff.

MULTIPLE METHODS

Tom Aspray

Tom Aspray specializes in foreign currencies.

Tom, how do you handle letting profits run?

That's something I use only in a trending market. When I see strong signs
of a trending move, I tend to give myself lots of room in terms of the stop.
Obviously, I also monitor the technical situation. You can't place a trade and
forget about it. I monitor every trade every day.

For example, if you have the ADX and ADXR basing for a couple of
months at the 20 level, followed by a move above 35, and they are rising at
a fairly rapid rate above the 35 level, that usually suggests a trending move.
We should see the ADX and ADXR move up to 50 plus. In that situation,
if you see a one- to two-day setback, it's usually an opportunity to add to
positions. The stop may seem uncomfortably wide, but experience suggests
that's when you can let profits run.

**Let's say you haven't reached trend mode yet. Would you be taking
profits at objectives then?**

If the daily analysis were positive but the weekly analysis were not positive, I would certainly be taking profits at objectives. I would stay in only if the weekly analysis suggested that a significant turn was occurring or had occurred.

I thought you said that the weekly indicators had to be looking good before you'd take a position.

That's when I'd look for a trending position. Normally what I do is take a position one-fourth or one-fifth of my normal size based on short-term analysis. If the weekly analysis was not turning into anything very significant, I would be looking to take profits at an objective on my short-term position.

How do you determine your short-term trade objectives?

I use Fibonacci retracement levels and point and figure methods to set my targets. I usually have trailing stops as well as price targets so that within the first or second day of a position my stop is probably at breakeven or higher.

Phyllis Kahn

Phyllis Kahn is a pure Gann trader.

Phyllis, where does letting profits run fit into your approach?

Because of my trading method, letting profits run is a pretty good thing to do.

Do you prefer trailing stops to setting price objectives?

Yes.

Do you ever use price objectives?

Oh, yes.

When?

I use Gann methods to generate objectives. Let's say you entered at a projected low turning point and the market ran for three or four days with big ranges and high volume. Now you've really got yourself a bottom. One of the things I do in advance is to calculate the difference between the most recent major high and low on the weekly or monthly chart. My first objective would be a one-third retracement of that difference. I will take profits at a one-third retracement. In a market like the S&P, you can get a one-third retracement in four or five days if you catch a big six-month low.

That means you let your profits run only to a one-third retracement. Then you take them.

In that case, yes. I would expect a reversal to occur and a reentry point to be established.

In what circumstances would you hold beyond the one-third retracement?

I remember an S&P trade off the October 1990 bottom. That trade was huge. It never looked back. It was a straight-up, spike move that went to an entirely higher level. I was able to hold that trade for almost a month, and it made about 7,000 points. That's an unusual occurrence off a very major bottom.

It's a matter of judgment as to when you take profits at a one-third retracement?

It's a matter of market action and judgment. When you have a market that's moving up vertically, you can use a trailing stop below the low of two or three days back and you never get stopped out. It holds you in using a simple trailing stop method like that. You don't have to judge. You sit and wait. Occasionally the market hands you some bonanzas like that.

When you have windfall profits, instead of using a stop two days back, use a stop below the low of the previous week so you're stretching your stop point. But always leave the stop in. You can distinguish a vertical market like that from a trading market.

In a vertical market, you let it go?

I try to. In normal circumstances you do get some kind of a reaction at the one-third retracement level. Even in the S&P. But occasionally you get these vertical moves, and you can recognize the difference.

Your primary tool for letting profits run is a pretty tight trailing stop below some previous low or above some previous high?

Yes, and it's always in the market. It's an open stop. I don't rely on putting the stop in every day. Never.

Steve Briese

Steve Briese is editor of the *Bullish Review* newsletter.

Steve, how do you let profits run?

Every trade should have a price objective. You set that objective based on the length of the trend you're trading. You can use an oscillator of half the length of the trend that you're trading. When that becomes overbought on a long trade (or oversold on a short trade), you want to exit a portion of the position. If you're only trading one contract, I suggest a different procedure, but hopefully you can take partial profits on your position at the price objective.

Based on the theory that one never picks tops well, you'd like to have some part of the trade continue to ride. Typically, every trend experiences a speculative blowoff. You'd like to take advantage of that. You do that by going to a trailing stop when you've reached your price objective. At that point place your trailing stop close behind the current price and trail it until you're stopped out. The key is never to move your stop away from the current price. You keep moving it a distance toward the price so you're stopped out somewhere near the end of the trend.

Once you reach your price objective, have the stop inside of one limit move so that you won't fail to get out the same day that the market reverses. You don't want to be locked in.

So your minimum trailing stop is less than one limit. And you're always moving your stop every day to respect that rule?

Yes. The biggest mistake you can make is setting your stops based on a longer-term trend just because the market starts going your way. In other words, don't change to a much higher profit target than you originally anticipated because the market starts moving in your favor. You must take part of your profits at your original price objective and begin using your trailing stop.

If the market is going to be explosive in your favor, it's going to be just as explosive when it reverses. If you leave your stop wide, typically those profits that you had already put in the bank mentally are going to disappear.

So you're willing to give up the monster, home run–type trades?

No, I'm not. If you're trading a short-term trend, you should have a re-entry point if you're stopped out before the move is over. You handle the longer-term trade with multiple entries. That's also the answer for the one-contract trader.

With two contracts, would you start out with the idea that your second contract is a longer-term trade and use a different objective and trailing stop?

It's very difficult for most people to trade multiple positions. Some do it all right. Some can trade around the position. That's fine.

What does that mean, "trade around the position"?

In other words, you have a long-term core position plus extra contracts to trade more short term. I know people who went long in the grain markets when my newsletter had major buy signals in August of 1992. They are still long [in 1994]. They have been holding distant contracts and rolling them forward. But they have taken profits on some of their positions on rallies. They took some profits and rebought on weakness. So trading around a position where you have a core long-term position and then trade a shorter cycle is a reasonable way to trade. You're trading two different trends. You can separate them.

Could you trade two contracts and take your initial position from the daily chart with the same stop on both and then if the trade is profitable, use objectives from the daily chart on your first contract and from the weekly chart on your second contract?

It's certainly permissible. I view it as trading two different trends. I would prefer to approach them with two different entry and stop calculations. There are times when you happen to buy two contracts trading a shorter trend. Then you discover it wasn't just the short-term trend that changed: the major trend reversed also. You can then shift one contract to a long-term trade.

Jake Bernstein

Jake Bernstein has written 27 trading books and has published his weekly MBH market letter for over 20 years.

Jake, how important to you is letting profits run?

It's the most important one of your four principles. But I'm tempted to say that every one of them is the most important one. I swear that if I had even one dollar for every time I took a profit too soon for no valid reason whatsoever, I'd be one hell of a lot richer.

When I take a look at some of the absolutely fantastic, incredible, up-and-down trends that we've had since I started trading and I see how little I took out of those moves by not letting profits run, it makes me sick.

That presupposes there would have been an objective way for me to hold those positions. But there are different ways, and that's what people should really trade for.

If it's true that markets are trendless most of the time, then it's also true that most systems are going to lose money in those trendless markets. When you finally do get hold of a good trade, why let it go so quickly?

One way to overcome that from a psychological standpoint is to put on a multiple-contract position. Then you can satisfy the part of you that says, "I need to bank some money. I've got to put some money in my pocket. I want to feel that green stuff and know that I'm trading well." If you depend on that kind of feedback, exit only part of your position so you can continue to ride the trend.

What methods do you use to let profits run?

There's no perfect way to let profits run other than forgetting you have a position. I remember an amazing experience I had in my early days of trading.

I bought some gold and took a quick profit on a few of the contracts. I forgot that I had a couple of contracts left. About eight months later my broker called and asked if I was going to get out because delivery was coming up. It was incredible. The gold market had moved about $15,000 per contract in my favor, and I didn't even know I had them.

My broker told me, "I've never seen anybody make as much money on one trade or hold a position for as long unless it was a loser. How did you do it?"

I said, "When I was first learning to trade, an old guy at the Board of Trade told me if you really want to make money and think the trend is going to be up, buy it, put it away, and forget about it. That's what I did."

Other than memory lapse, what's your favorite method of handling profitable trades?

The channel entry method I talked about in the previous discussion on trend following is a very simple method. It will keep you on the right side of the market if you've got a good trend.

That indicator consists of a moving average channel composed of a 10-bar moving average of the highs and an 8-bar moving average of the lows. The trend turns up when you have two successive price bars completely above the top moving average. It remains up until you have two successive price bars completely below the bottom moving average. Then the trend would be down. You would stay with profitable trades until the indicator reverses.

Most people end up with some kind of trailing stop strategy to let profits run. What do you think of that?

I'm not clear on this, but I think somebody at some point illustrated statistically that the traditional form of trailing stop doesn't work. Markets will find you if you're using a tight trailing stop.

You have to give the market enough leeway. I have made my biggest profits when I did not bump my stop up or down too quickly after the market moved in my favor. Markets need a lot of room, perhaps more nowadays than in the past because of the increased volatility caused by large funds and pools. A trailing stop is fine but not one that's too tight.

So you would trail your stop loosely and count on your system to get you out on a trend reversal before the market hit your stop.

Exactly. Another strategy is to change time frames. Here's what I mean. Let's say you entered a trade on a signal from a system using daily data. Let's say the market makes a big move in your favor. Then you can switch time frames to a shorter-term time frame like hourly data. Take a signal from that hourly data to go flat.

I thought you were going to say the reverse. We're talking about letting profits run. I thought you were going to say take a signal from daily prices and once you've got profits, then switch to weekly prices to get out. But you're saying the opposite—go the hourly. How is that going to let profits run? That's going to get you out sooner, isn't it?

This is for people who are in a situation where they have a big profit and are anxious and don't know what to do about their trailing stop. They want to have a tight stop but don't want to use a chart point because they know it probably won't work for them. They can switch to an intraday chart and run their system on the hourly chart.

Another method that makes a lot of sense to me is to buy an option on the other side of your trade. It will cost you a little bit of insurance money, but it's a form of protection.

You'd buy a put or a call as insurance?

If you're long a bunch and you've got a good gain on the market, you can take some of that profit and invest it in buying puts. They will probably expire worthless, but they will give you some protection in case the market does turn around.

And you don't get out soon enough.

Right. There's another important philosophical point at stake here. Most trading systems cluster between 40 and 50 percent accuracy. We know the random element in the market represents at least 40 to 60 percent of price activity. Therefore, it's not logical to look at every tick or to think that every tick or every chart formation has meaning. They don't.

There are too many traders trying to look at the markets from too stringent an analytical viewpoint. Most of what happens in the markets is meaningless. Why try to interpret every little movement, every little reversal, every little tick?

In trying to do too much, they're actually paying too much attention to the market. They're laboring under the Judeo-Christian work ethic that says, "If you're a good boy and you work hard and you pay a lot of attention, you're going to make a lot of money." I don't think that's true when you apply it to trading. There is a point of diminishing returns. You have to keep a certain distance from the market. Only then will you have the psychological resources to let your profits ride. You won't be looking at every tick and interpreting it in a fearful way.

LETTING PROFITS RUN NOT IMPORTANT

Stan Tamulevich

Stan Tamulevich is a very short-term trader and editor of *Marketline Update.*

Stan, because of your very short-term trading style, I assume that like trading with the trend, you don't think letting profits run is too important either.

No, I really don't. I try not to day trade, which means I'll look primarily for a two- or three-day opportunity. If you want to call that letting your profits run, then for me two or three days is letting my profits run.

You feel comfortable when there's a move in your favor for a couple of days to just take the profit and go on to the next trade?

Sure. My basic rule is if you really feel good about a position in those first two days, that's a good signal to take your profit. Otherwise, it usually comes back to haunt you when it goes the other way.

What's the longest trade you could have in terms of days? How long would it last?

In my last 19 trades, for example, the longest one lasted 11 calendar days. Ironically, that was a breakeven position. The market didn't want to move, so I juggled the stop around behind it. I never got a pop to take. It finally stopped me out.

What market was that?

It was oats, a real dynamite market. I suppose I could conceivably find myself in a position two or three weeks under optimum conditions.

Craig Solberg

Craig Solberg is editor of *Trade Winds* and strictly a weather trader.

Craig, how do you as a weather trader handle letting your profits run?

If you're trading the trend, you definitely should let your profits run. I try to do that as long as the weather forecast is in my favor. For example, assume we're in a very profitable trade in the soybean or corn market based on a drought situation where we're up a few thousand dollars per contract on some dry weather and the weather forecast still looks dry and very hot. Of course, we're going to let profits run as long as the weather forecast is in our favor.

But the minute that weather forecast changes, we're not going to simply move up our stop to protect profits. We're going to take profits immediately at the market. We know the weather is the full driving factor in that particular market at that time. If the weather is going to change, it's going to stop us out anyway, so we might as well just go ahead and take our profits. The bottom line is I'm going to let profits run on my position only as long as the weather forecast is in my favor.

That doesn't sound like the way other people let profits run. You're going to go with your weather forecast regardless of what the chart looks like or how far the market has moved.

If you don't know the weather forecast, you really have no business trading those kind of weather markets.

Have you found there were a number of situations over the years where you've really missed out on big moves because you let the weather shake you out too quickly and then you didn't get back in?

I would say definitely that is *not* the case. Let's assume we saw a weather forecast that would have a direct impact on the market, we got into a position in that market and were subsequently stopped out. If the market did turn around and go in our favor on that weather forecast, as long as the weather forecast were to stay the same and have the same impact on the market, we'd jump right back in. We might have missed some of the move when the market turned around, but if we believed the forecast's impact was still not discounted by the market, we'd jump right back in.

I hope the experts have stimulated some thoughts for your own profit protection tactics. In the next chapter, we'll examine the concept of managing risk, also known as money management. This key element is perhaps the least understood of the principles of successful trading.

CHAPTER 5

Manage Risk

Previous commodity trading literature has usually labeled the topics included in this chapter as *money management*. I think *risk management* is a more precise description of these concepts.

Most professionals agree that novices and amateurs spend far too much time studying entry techniques in relation to their true importance to successful trading. It is risk management, they agree, that really separates the winners and losers. Since the markets are not very predictable anyway, you can have a far greater impact on your bottom line by applying proper risk management techniques than by finding a new and better way to anticipate the next market top or bottom.

There is great popular misunderstanding about the riskiness of futures trading. The truth is that trading can be just as risky as you want to make it. While you can never control risk to the penny on each trade, you can easily determine the general level of risk over a year's time. By controlling your trading, you can limit risk to hundreds, thousands, tens of thousands, hundreds of thousands, or millions of dollars. The question is: Can you control yourself?

The most important way to control risk is by using initial protective stops. I covered how to implement protective stops in Chapter 3. Other ways include choosing not to trade certain markets, not trading during certain dangerous time periods, limiting the number of markets and contracts traded at any one time, and trading a diversified portfolio of markets and methods. Let's see how our experts employ these concepts.

Nick Van Nice

Nick Van Nice is editor of Commodity Trend Service's various systems and hotlines. He emphasizes long-term trading.

Nick, how do you manage risk?

I have a pretty simple approach to managing risk. There are two rules I use. One is never risk more than 2 percent of your account equity on any individual trade. The other is a monthly money management stop. It's a stop on you and your system. If during one month you lose more than 10 percent of your account equity as of any Friday close, you shut your system down until the next month.

You try to limit your losses to no more than 10 percent in a month?

That's right.

If you miss any entry signals in the meantime while you're waiting for the first of the next month to start trading again, that's just too bad.

Exactly. The monthly stop rule is best suited for CTAs or people who have to preserve and protect their track records. It's also good for anyone who wants to exercise control over his or her equity curve.

If you lose 10 percent in a month, do you close out all your open positions, too?

Yes. You close out all open positions and stop trading entirely until the next month. Then you start taking new signals again.

Whether you're a mechanical trader or more of a judgment trader, it serves two purposes. It sits you down while your system or subjective approach is out of tune with the markets. It gives everything a time to cool off. You let some time pass so the markets can change a little bit and maybe start accommodating your approach again.

What about other ways to manage risk, like your choice of the markets you trade?

It's very important to have good diversification. By picking one market from each of the several sectors of commodity futures, you can help control the volatility of your equity curve. Another way to say that is pick several markets to trade, preferably from different sectors.

Here's one way to do it. In the currencies, trade just the deutschemark. In the interest rates, trade one short-term instrument like Eurodollars and one longer-term instrument like T-notes. Moving to the energies, you would select maybe crude oil. Then select one market from the metals and so on. What I do is historically back-test all the markets and select the best performer from each sector. When you take that kind of portfolio approach, the equity curve is much more stable than if you traded one sector by itself.

If you have a $25,000 account, how do you decide how many markets you can trade?

We have a rule of thumb for the *Trendsetter* system. We suggest that your total initial margin requirements be no more than 20 percent of your account size.

So for a $25,000 account, you wouldn't want to trade more than $5,000 in margin? That can't be right.

It is right.

How many markets can you trade for only $5,000?

With a small account you should trade Mid-America markets. We're doing a lot of that these days. The currencies and interest rates pose the biggest problem to a small account. To be honest, I don't think someone with only a $25,000 account has any business trading a full T-bond or a full currency contract, period. There is too much risk.

The Mid-America deutschemark has very good liquidity. You can get in and out similarly to trading a full-size contract. It's the same with Mid-America T-bonds.

Even with a small account you can trade a full-size Eurodollar contract. They don't move that much. The same with gold. You're better off trading a full-size gold contract. We mix in Mid-America markets to help us get more diversification for our margin dollar.

How do you handle the situation when the margin changes? Do you constantly monitor margins and adjust your accounts?

No. You can start off with an initial margin of around 20 percent. That gives you a little buffer already. If margin requirements change a little bit, so be it. It's not that strict. As long as you're between 15 and 30 percent of account equity, you're in good shape.

What about individual risky events like crop reports and freeze seasons? Do you pay attention to them at all?

No. What I like to do is add commodities to a portfolio when the profit potential increases.

When does the profit potential increase?

Take the grains. I'll play the seasonals. I'll add corn or soybeans to the portfolio in the spring right before the crop goes into the ground. I know there's likely to be increased volatility. I don't know whether it will be up or down, but chances are you'll see more volatility in the soybean market from around April through harvest. I pick markets strategically based on seasonal factors. Heating oil can go into the portfolio late in the fall. And maybe I'll throw orange juice in there right ahead of the freeze season and coffee in early spring.

So you actually seek out markets that might be perceived to have increased risk.

Yes.

Would you trade them from the short side? For instance, would you trade orange juice from the short side during freeze season, or would you take only long positions at that point?

We take just the long signals. Wherever the profit potential is the greatest, that's what you trade. You have to apply a little bit of discretion, but generally where there's likely to be movement, that's where you want to be.

Colin Alexander

Colin Alexander is editor of *The Wellspring Futures Newsletter.*

Colin, how important is managing risk?

Many people consider this to be the most important trading principle of all. I would say it has roughly equal importance with trade selection but with a slight edge to trade selection. If, for the sake of argument, you commit 5 percent of your trading equity to any given trade and you don't have a handle on trade selection, after 20 consecutive losses, you would have nothing left.

I strongly believe in the final analysis that selection of markets to trade is even more important than capital management. An extension of that is to capitalize on markets that are moving for you by taking a decent-sized position. If you are trading in and out, it is not possible to make money consistently unless you are prepared to put up to a third of trading equity into a market that is really moving. Some examples are the collapse of soybeans last summer [1993], copper when it was falling apart in 1993, and Treasury bonds and Eurodollars this year [1994].

By that do you mean some kind of pyramiding approach?

Yes. What I like to do is take a small position initially. Then, if it starts working, I build up to a full weighting. A full weighting could be as much as one-third of trading equity.

Do you consider this to be part of managing risk?

Yes. Managing risk and managing capital are in my view exercises in handling the trade-off between potential reward and potential loss. When there is a real potential to make money, you must be adequately represented in a trade.

Do you employ any other risk management techniques other than limiting losses to 5 percent of trading equity? What about choice of markets as a method of managing risk?

I'm prepared to trade almost every popular market except lumber. I want to have sufficient liquidity.

What is enough liquidity?

I like to see total open interest of at least 5,000 contracts, which lumber doesn't have. I want some confidence that I can get out of a market if I am wrong, even at a certain cost. One of the advantages of stock indexes is that there is always some price at which you can get out.

What about crop reports? Do you pay any attention to those?

I tend to avoid staying with positions through major reports unless there's a profit cushion or unless the technicals are very strong. For example, I just liquidated a short position in live cattle because I didn't want to hold it through the Seven State Cattle on Feed Report. I also exited a short position in pork bellies because I didn't want to be short through the quarterly pig crop report.

What about diversification? Do you give any thought to that?

As a general rule, I don't like to see more than about one-third of my trading equity in one area of the board. Unless the merits of a situation are strong, I'd rather not trade than take a position just to achieve diversification.

Kelly Angle

Kelly Angle published a newsletter for many years. He currently manages money full-time.

Kelly, how do you approach managing risk?

I remember reading a book in my early days of trading that recommended risking no more than 10 percent of your equity on a single trade. It was one of W. D. Gann's books. After all my research and experience, I'm of the opinion that you don't have to risk more than a few percentage points per trade to earn triple-digit annual returns. Of course, the smaller your account, the smaller the dollar amount you can risk.

One reason I am now using $400 stops is it opens up opportunities for smaller accounts. My test figures show I can produce an annual return of more than 50 percent with a single-digit, worst-case drawdown using less than 1 percent of equity risk per trade. Traders should not underestimate the difference a small adjustment in risk can have on the risk/reward aspects of potential trading performance.

So the primary way you manage risk is to look at the percentage of your equity you're risking on each individual trade.

It never exceeds a particular threshold. When you use a fixed-dollar stop, the relative leverage you're using will constantly decline as your account increases through profits.

And that's what you want?

It's wonderful because it means you're less likely to give back your profits.

Does the percentage you want to risk change with the account size?

That's really a function of the account size.

If you have a $25,000 account, you're willing to risk, say, 2 percent. Whereas, if you have a $50,000 account, you'd rather risk 1 percent. Is that what you're saying?

I design our portfolios so that they will have a greater rate of return potential with a smaller account, but the drawdowns will be higher as well.

Because there's always a correlation between the percent return and the drawdown?

No. I used to think that, but I've decided it is an incorrect statement.

What's wrong with it?

It's true to a point. But there does not have to be a direct relationship between the two. The key to increasing return without increasing drawdown proportionally is relative leverage.

Relative leverage means how much you are risking per trade. If I have relative leverage of say 2° percent, then I should have a very good chance of producing greater than a 100 percent annual rate of return. My drawdown potential is going to be somewhere between 15 and 20 percent of equity. It may go as high as 30 percent at times. When I drop my relative leverage down to 1° percent and add limited diversification, I can reduce my drawdown potential without impacting my upside.

What kind of numbers are you shooting for?

Most $100,000 account holders in today's market environment would be happy with a 20 percent rate of return with drawdowns of less than 5 percent. They'd be tickled green over that.

If you had a $100,000 account, what percentage of your total equity would you like to risk on one trade?

I'd still be trading single contract positions with $400 stops. That equates to four-tenths of 1 percent.

Even with bigger accounts, you still like very small stops?

Yes. If someone wants a 50 percent rate of return, we can trade a $50,000 account with five markets and use twice the leverage—0.80 percent.

But with a $100,000 account you might trade 10 different markets and use less leverage.

That's correct. After talking with several thousand traders over the last 10 years, I have formed some conclusions about common risk profiles. Most of the people with $100,000 to $500,000 have different priorities than smaller account traders. Their priority is more what they can lose because they want to keep their money. Those with $25,000 or $50,000 seem to be more concerned about what they can make.

Would you say your entry method, which waits for low volatility in exchange for missing some moves, is a risk management technique?

I would think so.

What about other risk management ideas like diversification?

I've never seen a large rate of return generated from a small equity using a strategy of broad diversification. With accounts less than $100,000, a broad diversification strategy actually *increases* risk.

Why?

Because of what I call opportunity cost. Opportunity cost is something that no one ever thinks about or talks about, but it is the real cost of trading. Every time you put on a trade you take a risk. Too many different opportunities will bankrupt an account, especially a small one.

My dad's gold trade that made $100 million was based on one trading idea. George Soros is the only one I know in the world today who is trading $12 billion with that same approach. That's why he's done so well. He specializes with a large sum of money, and he's been rewarded handsomely for it. Most people don't have the nerve to do that. By the time they have $12 billion, they want to keep it.

Are you saying that the more markets you trade, the more marginal trades you have to settle for in order to trade the additional markets?

Right. People like the concept of diversification because it appears to reduce risk. However, it can prevent a small account from succeeding. Having too many poles in the water overturns a small boat.

If you pursue a strategy of less diversification, does that mean you trade only a few markets at a time but you look at the whole universe of possibilities? Or do you start by restricting yourself to a small number of markets and those are the only markets you trade?

I started with the idea that I wanted to trade one market for each $10,000 in account equity. I wanted to avoid trading sister markets in the same direction. Solving that problem has been difficult for small accounts. You can't trade three currencies and expect to contain risk. So you start picking and choosing. At any given time one currency might perform better than the others.

In testing what markets to trade, you run the same risk of overoptimizing that you run in testing entry and exit rules. I designed my entire *Cornucopia* system before I tested anything. If a concept works the first time you test it, that's the best safeguard against overoptimization. I predetermined which markets made sense to trade at each $10,000 equity level based on historical volatility, liquidity, and volume.

So you do restrict yourself to particular markets for a particular account, and those are the only markets you trade. You don't look at the whole universe and decide from day to day which different market you're going to trade next.

Right. There are three sectors that are permanent segments of the portfolio. They are bonds, currencies, and stock indexes (the NYFE for small accounts). I don't incorporate a flexible portfolio until the account is above $30,000. Then I add two markets from an evolving universe selected from the most active markets. Next I add two more markets on top of those.

But on a smaller account you're stuck. If the two markets you pick don't trend, you're out of luck.

I wait for the market to come to me. I haven't seen a period since I started trading in 1980 where the interest rate and currency complexes weren't represented in the top portion of my volatility index. So I know those markets will be moving. If the universe should change, then I guess I'll go back and reassess.

What about other risk management ideas like avoiding crop reports and freezes. Do you pay any attention to that or do you just figure if you're trading a market you trade it and that's it?

I've eliminated all that. I even stopped worrying about evening sessions. I don't trade Globex because I didn't test my system that way. I trade it exactly like I tested it.

Most system traders, although not all, ignore the nighttime sessions.

The big managers don't. They're in there with their systems trading all night. You can see the market action. Trading just the day session is about 7 hours of a 24-hour market. It's like having your satellite dish go down 66 percent of the time. When you think about the big managers trading cash with a 24-hour desk, it can be pretty scary in terms of what you might be missing out on or exposing yourself to.

You run the risk of being caught in a gap opening, but at the same time you avoid the times you would needlessly have been stopped out overnight. That more than makes up for the potential risk you might face with an overnight gap.

I agree.

Russell Wasendorf

Russell Wasendorf is a broker, money manager, and editor of *Futures Factors.*

Russ, let's talk about managing risk.

Managing risk is extremely important, but it can also be such an inhibiting factor that it may not be totally compatible with the futures markets. By that I mean managing risk is a subjective characteristic. To give you an example, my typical position (original entry position) in the grain markets is usually 100,000 bushels. That's a comfortable risk level for my capitalization. But for someone else, it may be too much. So managing risk becomes a subjective factor.

Managing risk can become a restricting factor for beginning traders or traders who are not well capitalized. Markets are indeed risky. You must recognize the riskiness, and the only way you can comfortably manage some of the risk is to be well capitalized.

Having said that, I still accept the importance of managing risk from the perspective of making sure that stops are always in the market and following my system to the letter without deviating. Managing risk also means you don't take profits early because taking profits early loses an opportunity, which is also a risk factor. You best manage risk by diversifying your positions rather than trying to be too protective of each individual position.

If you need to be well capitalized to accept the inherent risk in futures trading, what's the minimum somebody should have to start trading?

I did a very intriguing study back in 1980. Conti Commodities hired me as a consultant to come in and study the performance of accounts within their firm. We studied the size of the original account and determined whether or not these individuals made money after a year of trading.

I broke it down into accounts that started at $5,000, $10,000, $25,000, $50,000, and $100,000. Starting with a $5,000 account, after one year 95 percent of the customers had lost money. The percentage declined as the amount of money invested increased. At a $50,000 original investment, there was a 50 percent chance the individual would make money after a year. At $100,000 the percentage turned positive for the investor. It's my conclusion that those numbers suggest you shouldn't be trading the futures markets without at least $100,000 in your account.

Do you think the sophistication of the individual involved rather than just the size of the account had anything to do with success? Did you try to isolate that?

There was no way we could determine sophistication. Traders tend to be more sophisticated today than they were in 1980, but I don't think those percentages have changed a whole lot since.

That's a sobering concept. It says a lot to people who don't have much money.

It does. It also applies to professional money managers. I manage a data base with about 660 CTAs in it. CTAs who accept less than $100,000 on average perform more poorly than CTAs who require more than $100,000.

Do you consider things like crop reports and freeze seasons in trying to manage risk? Or do you figure they are part of the risk in the markets and just trade right through them?

It's my firm belief that the marketplace itself already builds all those factors into the price. Futures trading is a zero sum game. There is a buyer and seller in each transaction. The only thing that moves the price is the aggressiveness of the buyers and sellers. The news is going to be pretty much in the market. If you observe price, you are observing the composite opinion of everybody who is involved.

If you short the orange juice market during freeze season, you subject yourself to a series of limit moves that could upset your risk control. Are you saying that if you have enough money in your account, limit moves are not really a problem?

In today's market limit moves are almost a nonconsideration. If you look at the pattern of price action over the last five years, limit moves other than in the livestock markets are not significant. Limit moves are often exaggerated by restructuring the limit. If you are concerned about a 30-cent limit move in soybeans, tomorrow that limit is going be 40 cents or 60 cents or nonexistent. So your capitalization is going to be your most important protection.

Bill Gary

Bill Gary is editor of the CIS *Price Perceptions* newsletter.

Bill, how important is managing risk to successful trading?

I would say it is pretty important. Here is an example. Most people trade more than one market at a time, so it is critical to look at risk exposure from an overall account standpoint. Evaluate your stops in terms of all your positions. I actually run this through a computer every day to know what my absolute total risk exposure is. When carrying large risk exposure, I have never been stopped out of all my trades at one time, but there's always that possibility. Thus, maximum risk exposure should never be more than half your total capital.

As long as it isn't more than half, are you content to add new positions?

Yes.

If you also have some profitable positions, would you include those as a credit that you would subtract from your risk?

Right.

You compute the amount of risk to the stop for all your positions and then calculate the total net risk?

Right. We see where the market closed the previous day and where our stops are this morning. We net out all positions and add that to our previous day's equity.

What do you do if your risk is too large?

I try to reduce it. I look at the positions. Are there any I can close out or on which I can move stops closer? If there are any in the latter stages of a move, then I might move or change the trailing stop and make it tighter. As a general rule, my stops are based on market action. I prefer to let the market tell me what to do rather than making a subjective decision just to reduce risk. Another possibility is substituting options for futures positions.

Do you believe in diversification?

No. I don't attempt purposefully to diversify. I know many traders do, but my philosophy is I would rather be concentrated in fewer markets. I like to diversify up to about five or six markets, but not any more than that.

Why?

Because, number one, I'd be spreading myself too thin. Number two, the money people make in the markets is not by extreme diversification. Who would go to a horse race and bet on all 10 horses? If you're going to have a worthwhile return trading commodities, you've got to put a larger proportion of your eggs in some basket along the way. I believe I can do a better job by concentrating on fewer markets, knowing more about them, and trading them better.

Do you pay attention to crop reports or freeze seasons?

Yes, I do, but not to control risk. I look for exceptional opportunities. For instance, there is a very strong seasonal trend to have a corn and soybean rally in the May–July period every year. That's attributable to the planting period and the uncertainty that goes along with it.

It is not a great risk to go long during a seasonal up period. What I'm talking about is the risk in going *opposite* the seasonal trend. For instance, to be short orange juice in the winter. Many people might say, "No, I don't want to be short orange juice in the winter or short cattle through a Cattle on Feed Report because there's too much danger of a bunch of limit up moves against me."

I don't enter the market based on an upcoming report. If my analysis is correct and if my technical work is good, if a report is going to be negative to my position, I'll be stopped out either before or just after that report. Usually, I have already solved what the report should be and how the markets should react to it. So I'm not afraid to hold positions through reports. In fact, probably half of our money over a period of a year is made by holding positions through these reports and being on the right side.

We seldom have those kind of run-up moves any more, where you're locked in. The reason is you can buy options to protect yourself. The availability of options has taken most of that kind of volatility out of the marketplace.

Are there any other ways you manage risk?

I do use options. For instance, right now we've got a major grain report coming out. It's going to be the key report for old crop grains for the rest of this crop season. I realize that it has the potential to be a bearish report, but I have a bullish bias on the market. I have a bullish bias from fundamental analysis and from the market's seasonal attributes. The thing that's against me is the intermediate trend. It's down. So if I want to take a position, I may take part or all the position in options to start with. That way I know what the risk is and it is absolutely limited. After the report I convert those options to futures positions. If it's extremely favorable, I can just buy futures and keep the options.

Stan Tamulevich

Stan Tamulevich is editor of *Marketline Update*, which is geared to smaller accounts.

Stan, how important is managing risk to your trading style?

It is important. As an advisory service you never really talk about managing risk. You ignore it out of necessity. You're an idea person. You're always giving ideas to people.

In my estimation you have to be really conservative when you play this game. By design my style is to say, "I'm not going to lose over 10 percent of my equity on any trade." That's the maximum to which I want to expose myself. Generally less. Before I take a trade, I know how I want to enter it and I know how much I'm going to risk when I get into the trade. I don't use a formula, but when I look at that risk in terms of dollars, I want to keep it in the 5 to 10 percent range. Since my trades are short term, I'm rarely committing more than 50 percent of my equity in total positions.

If you apply that 5 to 10 percent risk limit and you consider that I'm in a trade for two to three days, the only way to risk a lot of equity is to have an abundance of good ideas. My ideas don't flow that readily. I may have 15 trades a month on the outside. Consequently, if they're only two to three days in duration, I won't be using much equity in the account. One day I'll wake up and have five ideas that I ought to implement. I am in a position where, in that situation, I can take them all.

Certainly one of the ways you must manage risk is by the markets you trade. You wouldn't trade all the markets because some of them are a little too wild.

That's right. I am a little shy about trading the currencies, although I do take some currency trades. If I see a T-bond idea, I might gravitate toward T-notes instead. An alternative is to trade mini-contracts on the Mid-America Exchange. I have had great success with fills trading those. There is no problem in those markets.

What Mid-America markets do you trade?

I have traded the currencies and the bonds there. The full-size grain contracts are already small. You don't have to think about Mid-America grains unless you have a very small account.

Do you trade the meats?

I do, but I consider the regular contracts to be small enough.

I assume you don't trade the stock indexes at all.

Occasionally, I will. My style makes it pretty tough because the exposure is significantly larger than the other markets. If I were to trade the stock indexes, my month would either be a super winner or super loser depending on how I did with them.

With your approach wouldn't trading the NYFE be worthwhile? It's a poorly trending market overall. There would be lots of back and forth action consistent with your short-term style.

I've had good luck calling the turns in the NYFE in the intermediate term, but my close stops have hurt me.

What about things like crop reports and freeze seasons? Do you pay attention to those?

Yes, I do. I don't get in their way. Some people, like Larry Williams, say you can ignore them and everything will iron out. It's my contention that you shouldn't hold a position through a report, particularly a quarterly pig report. Those things are dynamite.

When you're risking as little as you are on each trade, you can't afford that kind of exposure.

Absolutely. You may find yourself in a position where you're at risk for a couple of limit moves. By design, you're trying to risk no more than 50 points in hogs. A couple of 150-point limits will blow you away.

What other situations like crop reports do you stay away from?

That's one of the reasons I'm shy on the bonds and currencies, because many of the monetary reports have a significant effect on them.

Are there any other ways you manage risk?

It would be easy to overtrade using my approach. You might want to go for broke on some idea. It's important, particularly for a beginning trader, that you tread lightly to conserve capital for the long haul.

If you're worried about overtrading, what about some limit on the number of trades you take—for example, not taking more than one trade a day or two trades a week on average. Have you ever thought about that?

That's a terrible idea. There are some days when I have three or four good ideas. If I attempted to select which trade was best, I guarantee you I'd pick the wrong one every time. I must take every good trade I see.

Is there no limit?

No. If I see four or five trades, I'll take them, even if they involve committing 80 percent of my equity. The odds are I'm going to be stopped out on one of them the first day. I'll probably be out of the rest within three days anyway. If I did have four or five positions going, it would be very unlikely that I'd find two or three more the next day.

You naturally limit yourself.

Sure. It's probably a psychological thing. If you have four or five positions, you don't look as hard for additional trades because you want to do a good job managing what you already have. You concentrate your efforts on doing that rather than trying to find something new.

Robert Miner

Robert Miner is editor of the *Major Market Analysis Report.*

Bob, how important is managing risk in your approach.

Risk, by definition, is the probability of an event happening that endangers money. The stop-loss order is the vehicle for setting the maximum capital exposure on any given trade. I decide where to place my protective stops using the same methodology I use to enter.

Do you have a certain limited universe of markets that you follow?

About five or six. The main ones are gold, T-bonds, and soybeans. I follow the S&P in the newsletter, but I don't personally trade it. I track the currencies, especially deutschemarks. I trade them every now and then. There are a number of others I look at and if something stands out, I analyze it more closely. One of those, for instance, is sugar. I've currently been long sugar for about six weeks. That's because it had a chart pattern that was just screaming. I never trade meats. The only grain is soybeans. That's about it. There are really only about five or six markets I regularly analyze.

But that's not because you are managing risk. It's an analysis issue.

Right. I'm looking for the markets that will meet all my conditions to make a trade. I rarely have a trade on in more than two different markets at a time. It's usually just one.

Is that because your analysis methods are so complicated you can't keep track of that many markets?

Oh, no. I follow six markets in about 15 minutes a day.

Then why do you limit yourself to so few markets?

Why would I need more? There's almost always a trade available when I'm following just those few. I know those markets well because I've been watching them day by day for so long.

Do you prefer to trade more contracts in a few markets than fewer contracts in many markets?

Yes.

If you had a big account, you wouldn't trade any more markets. You'd just trade more heavily in the markets you follow.

Right. All any market is to me is numbers—bars on a chart. I'm looking through my charts to see which one is setting up according to my analysis. That's the next trade I'll take. The name on the chart doesn't mean that much. If you have five or six markets that tend to move fairly regularly, at any given time one of them is almost always ready to trade.

Do you have any rules for the maximum risk exposure in your account?

The maximum is 5 percent of equity on any one trade.

You don't care how many trades you put on as long as you're not risking more than 5 percent on each one.

Right.

If you were going to pyramid, you still wouldn't want to risk more than 5 percent on the total position.

Correct.

What about crop reports and freeze seasons? Do you pay any attention to those?

No.

So your risk management is primarily through stop-loss orders. That's the only kind of risk management you bother with.

Yes. The risk is expressed by the confidence you have in your analytical methodology and trading strategy. Hopefully, it's right more times than it's wrong. If it is, and you keep your losses limited when you are wrong, you will come out all right in the end.

Don't you believe in diversification?

I've never understood the attraction to diversification. To me that's just saying you don't know what any of the markets are going to do so you throw everything at the wall and hope something sticks.

Yes, that sounds like a good description of my humble philosophy.

Peter Brandt

Peter Brandt is a long-time professional trader and editor of *The Factor* advisory service. He specializes in trading classical chart patterns and uses very small stops.

Peter, what is your approach to managing risk?

That expression will have different meanings to different people. But as I view risk management, it is the single most important component of successful trading. Risk management concepts are more important in my view than how you generate trading signals. Risk management deals with such questions as what percent of my capital am I going to risk on a given trade.

What's the answer to that?

I don't like risking any more than 1 percent. At times 2 percent if certain things come into play. In an extremely outrageous situation, which doesn't happen very often, maybe 3 percent. But no more than that.

Since you use small stops, do you get up to that threshold by trading multiple contracts?

That's correct. Another risk management question is how do you handle important government reports that you know are likely to have a big effect on a market.

How do you handle those?

There aren't that many reports that I pay attention to. There are some, and there are important events, too. There's only one a month, and it's some government report that the market tends to focus on. I don't know what's coming right now. It's probably unemployment. But if I have a big position on and I'm going into that report without a profit in my trade, I'm likely to lighten up.

Another risk management issue is how do you handle highly correlated markets. If I'm going to risk 2 percent in T-bonds, what do I do if I also see great signals in Eurodollars and T-bills at the same time. I may also have signals in 5-year notes, 10-year notes, and muni bonds. If you are in four or five correlated markets and take your 2 percent risk on each one, all of a sudden you're risking 10 percent on the total situation. That's an important element of risk management: understanding the correlation between markets—whether they're going to move together.

Do you treat correlated markets as one trade for risk management purposes?

I'll extend it a little bit, but not much. In general, I consider it a single position. If I'm going to be wrong in notes, I'm going to be wrong in bonds.

What about how many total positions you can have in an account at once?

That has never really been a consideration for me. If someone is trading to the point where they're getting a margin call, they're overtrading. But I don't think it's important.

Why, because you don't trade that much?

I doubt if I've ever been over 50 percent margined.

If you're risking only 1 or 2 percent, you can have quite a few positions, and the risk doesn't become too steep.

That's right.

What about markets you select to trade? Are there markets you don't like for risk reasons?

Oh, yes. I've had some terrible experiences with fills in some markets.

When you are getting bad fills, what you have tried to define as your risk isn't necessarily what you'll end up losing. You're risking substantially more because of the low liquidity. Of course, what we might consider a thin market is never too thin when we're right. It's only too thin when we're wrong. For markets like natural gas, platinum, and lumber, when I determine my position size, I'm going to consider my success in getting good fills.

What about the S&P? Isn't it hard to trade the S&P with your usual stops [in the $300 range]?

I don't trade the S&P.

Why not?

Because I can't trade it with that kind of stop.

So that would be one that you would eliminate for risk management reasons also.

Right.

Any other popular markets you don't trade for risk management reasons?

I generally don't trade livestock, but I think that's for technical reasons more than risk management reasons.

They don't respond well to your methods?

That's right. Pork bellies will at times, but generally I have not found the meats to be very good charting markets. So I just leave them alone and let somebody else trade them.

Like the First Lady.

I've never found wheat to be a particularly good charting market. So I look at any signal I see in wheat with a jaundiced eye.

Any other risk management ideas?

Yes. Where a person has the ability to use overnight stops in foreign exchange markets, it's probably wise. There are such huge moves that take place overnight, particularly in the yen. When we're sleeping is when it's most actively traded. I don't mean the Globex. I will use the overnight markets to do EFPs (exchange for physical) in the currencies.

Craig Solberg

Craig Solberg is editor of *Trade Winds.* He specializes in weather-related trades.

Craig, where does managing risk fit into your approach?

It ties closely to cutting losses short, your second principle. It's difficult to envision anyone being a good trader without understanding something about managing risk. The first thing I learned when I started in the commodity field was good money management. Some studies have shown that of every 10 traders, only one is profitable or something like that. That relates directly to the general lack of good risk management.

What is that axiom? There are a lot of old traders, but there aren't many old and bold traders.

When you get into a trade, you must have a specific risk in mind. When the market reaches a particular level you have to say to yourself, "Okay, I was wrong about the trade. Let's get out right now with this limited loss and live to fight another day." You can't stay with a market in the hope that it will finally come around to your perspective.

When you enter a trade, it should be on your own terms at a price level where it appears to be a good economic value for the market. Before you place your order, determine a reasonable level to risk if the market goes against you. If a trade is losing money, it's not reacting to the fundamentals as you thought it would. When the price reaches that level, you must admit to yourself that you were wrong about the market.Take your loss there. That's the bottom line.

You must manage your risk to allow yourself to participate in the next big move. Just because you lost on this trade doesn't mean the next one is not going to be one of the biggest winners ever.

On the other side of the coin, just because you made $2,000 or $3,000 per contract on your last trade, that does not give you the right to be extremely bold on the next one. I've been guilty of that. Many times after a series of very good winning weather trades, I have the tendency to want to risk a little more on the next trade than I would have otherwise. You may be a winner today, but you can turn right around and lose most of your profits tomorrow.

When you're trading weather markets, you're jumping in and out in the middle of highly volatile situations. Many people would say, "Gosh, when the market's that volatile, I'm afraid to trade at all." You say, "Boy, this is just when we want to be in there, when the weather is making things go up, down, up." Doesn't that make it more difficult to manage risk?

I try not to jump in and out. As long as the weather forecast stays the same, I stay with my position. But that's really the nature of the beast. If you're going to be a weather trader like I am, you should look forward to situations like that because those are the times where the market is playing to your hand. You have to be able to talk the talk and walk the walk.

Under those conditions the market could care less about any of the other fundamentals. It wants to know what the weather forecast means. The chart picture may appear extremely volatile with gaps and limit moves both ways, but if you look at it from a weather forecast perspective, you can see exactly why the market did everything it did over a week or a month or even a year-long period.

Courtney Smith

Courtney Smith is editor of the *World Investment Strategic Edge* newsletter.

Courtney, how important is money management in your approach?

I emphasize the psychological aspects as most important, but the second most important consideration is money management. When you have a series of losing trades, you must retain enough equity to stay in the game so your system or method will have an opportunity to win. When you go through that bizarre circumstance where you have 10 consecutive losing trades, it won't

Courtney Smith

Courtney Smith is currently president and chief investment officer of Pinnacle Capital Management, Inc. Pinnacle manages portfolios for institutions and individuals. Portfolios are invested in stocks, fixed income, and derivatives in many currencies. Its sister company, Pinnacle Capital Strategies, Inc., provides managed futures accounts.

He is the editor of *World Investment Strategic Edge* newsletter. This investment advisory newsletter is highly ranked over the last three years by *Commodity Traders Consumer Report* for futures trades, and according to Smith, the stock portfolio has consistently outperformed the stock market with less risk.

Smith is the author of five books, including *Profits Through Seasonal Trading, Commodity Spreads, How to Make Money Trading Stock Index Futures, Seasonal Charts for Futures Traders,* and *Option Strategies.*

Recently, he was president and chief executive office of Quantum Financial Services, Inc., a $100 million futures and stock brokerage firm. He was first vice president and treasurer of the New York branch of Banca della Svizzera Italiana (BSI), a Swiss bank. He was previously group vice president in charge of financial derivatives at the French bank Banque Paribas, New York, and was vice president and director of Futures Research and Commercial Services for Paine Webber, Inc.

Mr. Smith has been a featured speaker at investment conferences throughout North America and Europe. He has appeared many times on television shows such as *Wall Street Journal Report* and *Moneyline,* as well as other shows on CBS, CNN, and FNN. He is often a featured guest on CNBC.

Write to him at Pinnacle Capital Management, Box 7603, New York, NY 10150-7603. Telephone (212)-832-0532.

mean that much because you will be able to keep playing the game. If you keep playing the game, eventually you should win.

Do you have any rules of thumb for that?

I will never risk more than 1 percent of my equity in any given trade. I would really prefer to keep it below one-half of 1 percent. I calculate that on the current equity I'm trading.

It requires a lot of equity to trade that way, doesn't it?

It does. Either that or extremely tight stops, which means you can have a lot of losers.

What about the guy who has only $10,000. How can he trade using 1 percent stops? All he can risk is $100.

He can trade mini-contracts or spreads. Realistically, he's probably going to have to go to 2 percent. Remember also the 1 percent rule applies to current equity. A person who starts with $100,000 can risk $1,000 on his first trade. If he loses, now he can risk only 1 percent of the $99,000 he has left. And so on and so forth. That way, by definition, you're always going to have some money left.

Money management is a critical element. I look at everything from a money management perspective. I first determine the optimal stop. Then the number of contracts I trade is simply the amount of money I am able to risk with my 1 percent rule or the ° percent rule, divided by the amount per contract I'm risking on that particular trade. I try to have as tight a stop as possible because then I can trade the most contracts.

Do you use money management stops? Do you use chart stops? What do you use?

Right now I'm using exclusively chart stops. But in the past I've used mechanical system stops, and I'll probably use them again in the future.

That's not a money management stop.

No. The money management comes in the size of the position.

How small is the tightest stop that's reasonable?

A couple hundred bucks. I just got stopped out for a $150 loss.

In?

Copper. I was looking for it to collapse if the trade was good. And it wasn't, so I lost $150. I'll risk up to as much as $1,200, but I prefer keeping it in the low hundreds.

James Kneafsey

James Kneafsey has been a major money manager since 1977.

Jim, how do you manage risk?

The key part for us is the ratio of average profitable trade to average losing trade. If you can have as high as possible average-gain-to-average-loss ratio, then you have a great system or a great trading method. Next, we control our risk on each trade starting the first day. Every trade has a money management loss maximum during the first couple of days until the system's parabolic trailing stop can catch up with it. Controlling the absolute risk on each trade is very important. The question of how many positions you put on for a certain size account is a whole separate area of risk management.

Let's take those ideas one at a time. How do you determine your money management risk? Is that in relation to the commodity or in relation to the account or something else?

Purely the commodity. We use a five-year window to look at what the maximum gains and losses have been from entry point to exit point trading our system. How many times have we had gains of $5,000, $4,000, $3,000, and so on. We list the losses the same way. The losses range from $500 on the low end to $2,500 on the high end with the S&P. Most are in the $500 to $1,000 range.

How do you decide whether your stop is going to be, say, $500 or $1,000?

We look at the average loss per trade that our system experienced in the last five years. We also look at the drawdown. We try to roughly match the average loss that the system generates. We also add some buffer around that, based on standard deviations, to allow for market noise that might carry you beyond the average loss. For example, oats is in the $500 range, whereas platinum is $1,000.

So the idea is that the average loss of your system gives you some rough idea of how volatile the market is within the trend.

Right. The average loss in corn may have been $295, but we picked $500 somewhat arbitrarily as our minimum stop-loss. The average loss in platinum, for example, is $620, and that's roughly twice the corn loss. So we use a $1,000 stop in platinum versus $500 in corn. Another way of saying that is everything is geared to our lowest common denominators, which are corn and oats.

The next risk management method you listed was the number of positions in relation to your account size.

Yes, and how much diversification you want in the account. In the past we've had four kinds of accounts. We've had diversified accounts, a metals-only account, a currency account, and what we call financials, which are currencies, interest rates, and stock index futures. It also depends on the size of the account you're dealing with. Is it a $25,000, $50,000, $100,000, or $1 million account?

When we had them, we traded all $25,000 accounts the same way to keep it consistent because we were dealing with different brokerage firms.

Don't you react negatively to the idea of somebody having a metals-only account?

Yes.

I assume you did it for marketing reasons, but it's not a good idea, is it?

No, it's not. We did it with Jim Sinclair in the early 1980s. It was indeed a marketing ploy.

With an always-in-the-market system, you must have fairly rigorous ideas about what markets you will trade and what group of markets you will trade with what size accounts.

I have a slight asterisk to put here. In the last three years we have been managing strictly currency accounts and strictly hedge accounts and strictly institutional accounts and also using options. That's why we're always in the market because with hedging we have to protect ourselves no matter what happens. The truth is there's a speculative element in all hedging accounts because you're making buy-and-sell decisions all the time. You have to go both ways. You can't lose money when the dollar moves down and you have to make money when it goes up.

Let's talk about an institutional account that is a large commodity account. How do you use diversification as a risk management tool with that type of account?

For the broad-based commodity account we try to have as many commodity groups represented as possible and a number of liquid commodities within each group.

How do you decide how many contracts are too much?

We try to balance each of the six groups with respect to the risk exposure and the expected returns of that particular group.

What are your six groups?

Agriculture and livestock, currencies, metals, interest rates, stock index futures, and foods.

Do you want to have roughly equal representation from all six?

Yes. In some groups you're going to have bigger trend moves than others, but it represents a very reasonable form of diversification.

Within the groups, do you try to balance the various markets?

Exactly.

Is there some limitation in terms of the amount you'll trade, say, for every $100,000 in the account? How do you determine that?

Yes. We would never exceed using 50 percent for margin. In fact, we usually have been below 50. Normally, in the 40 or 50 percent range, but never over 50 unless there was some sudden increase in margin.

For risk management purposes are there some markets you won't trade?

Yes.

Why?

Because they're too illiquid.

Do you have a limit in terms of the open interest or volume you want to see?

It's not absolute, but we certainly want to see more than 300 contracts of volume per day and total open interest of more than 2,000.

So you would trade lumber for instance.

Yes, it does fit within those guidelines. Ironically though, we have never traded lumber. The reason is we never could get our fundamental analysis to work on lumber because it's such a bizarre industry. Typically we do not trade orange juice or palladium.

Orange juice has plenty of open interest and volume.

The volume dips below 300 during some summer months.

What about individual situations in various markets like crop reports and freeze season? Do you pay any attention to that kind of thing?

I think those things smooth out over time. If you decide to be out of the markets before the reports come along, they're coming along every day. I think that's a losing proposition. The technicals of the market already encompass, in many cases, the results of these reports. I think you follow your system and ignore the reports. You have to accept that your system will end up on the wrong side of the market in some cases.

If you're going to trade cattle, you trade it through the reports?

Yes.

Anything else under risk management?

For a new trader, the key is to decide the total amount you're willing to risk and stick to that. If you lose it, do what the professional traders do and go into the penalty box for awhile. Sit on the sidelines and see what mistakes you made before you come back in.

That's an overall cutoff point.

Yes. Very few people do that, by the way. It is a form of discipline. Pick your cutoff point before you start. In other words, if you have $10,000 to put in the market, you can decide to stop trading if you lose $5,000. If you have the misfortune of losing the $5,000, stop and try to figure out what went wrong. Most people just race along and lose more. If you lose 50 percent of your investment capital in a short period of time, your system is not working right or you're doing something else that is very wrong.

If it took a long period of time, that wouldn't be too good either.

That's probably worse.

You wasted your time for a longer period.

If you're going to lose 50 percent, it's better to do it quickly. Actually, I have done it myself.

Walter Bressert

Walter Bressert was one of the original cycle gurus in the early 1970s. He currently markets a cycles trading software program.

Walt, how important is managing risk to overall trading success?

Controlled risk is what I call it. You always control your risk. You always control the market. You always control your entry. Therefore, it's always managed. It's always under your control.

You decide what your trading strategy is. You decide when you're going to get into the market because you've got a dollar risk you can live with, you've got a profit objective you can live with, you've got three different time frames and three profit objectives. In other words, you've got a trading strategy.

You must do the homework to be in control of all three of those. As a trader, when you get into the market you should know at what point you're going to admit you're wrong. You should know what strategies you're going to use to have the market take you out.

Theoretically, you're in complete control. Realistically, you're still dealing with fear and greed. There's no way around those, but you should strive to be balanced. The most important part of risk management for me is being balanced. When I go out of balance, I'm making bad decisions because I'm suddenly not in control.

My approach to risk management is to eliminate as much of the fear and greed as possible by eliminating as much judgment as possible. I use a structured approach that allows me to control how much I'm going to lose if I'm wrong and be in control of how much I'm going to make if I'm right.

My method tries to buy near the bottom of the weekly cycle, then uses the smaller daily trading cycle to buy dips on the way up. The opposite applies in a bear market. You should take advantage of the short-term moves by taking quick profits on one of the three contracts. Usually it's $500 to $1,000, and it's within about five market days. That way you have money in your pocket right away. You're balanced psychologically and that money in your pocket offsets a sizable portion of the risk exposure for the remaining two contracts. When you're not at risk, you think differently. When not at risk, you're balanced. Risk management to me is being in control and being balanced.

You don't like to risk more than about 2 or 3 percent of your equity on your total three-contract position.

No more than 5 percent is what usually pops up. But if I can get it for 2 or 3, I'll grab it.

So one way you manage risk is the relationship of the individual position to your total account. Do you have any limitations on the number of different positions you'll take in the whole account?

I don't have any particular limitation on the number of positions that I will trade. Just by the nature of the markets and the way I trade, I'm not going to be able to trade more than three to five markets at one time. I'm only going to put on positions that allow me to risk no more than 5 percent of my equity. That limits me to some extent. I'm not going to risk more than 20 percent of my equity on any one market group at any one time. That limits me.

What I set out to do is develop a large number of entry patterns so that I can get into the market and take off my short- and intermediate-term positions and hold on to the long-term position for the bigger move. I'm trying to identify big moves that are coming, position myself with as many entries as possible, take off two-thirds of the contracts as quickly as possible, and hold the remainder for the bigger move. I go into the market with 5 percent risk, and that risk should be reduced to about 1$\int$ of a percent in five days if I can take my number one contract off at a dollar amount that approximates the risk.

Is that your risk on that one position or is that your total three-contract risk?

It's my total three-contract position.

Are you trying to make enough on your first trade to cover the total loss that you would have taken on your three-contract position?

I'm trying to make enough profit on the first trade to cover the total loss for one contract out of the three I'm trading. To make it simple assume I'm risking 6 percent. Each contract has a 2 percent risk. If I can make 2 percent on that first contract, I eliminate the 2 percent risk on that contract by closing it out, plus the 2 percent profit I take offsets the 2 percent risk of another contract I still have. My total exposure is down to 2 percent. Now I'm balanced, and I have money to look for my next entry pattern. Doing that I can build up a fair amount of positions as the market is getting ready to move.

Is diversification important to you as a risk management tool? You said you would risk 20 percent per group. That would seem to allow you to trade four different markets in one group at one time.

That doesn't mean I'm going to get into the same group at the same time. I would not have more than 20 percent of my money at risk in open profits if I were stopped out in a group. I diversify if the market allows me to. If I see a move coming, I will focus a tremendous amount of energy into beans, for example. I will put a lot of money in beans. If I see something that's an offset in cattle or silver or gold or another market, I'll trade that market as well. I am not able to trade more than three to five markets. I can't keep track of them.

Some people try not to take more than one position in one group at a time. Then they try to diversify into other groups. That's what we were asking about. You're not concerned about that. You're more interested in whether you have a good entry pattern.

I'm not interested in a systematic approach that follows 10 or 15 markets and always has me spread across them. I want to identify the moves that are likely to occur and apply my talents towards what I think is a big move coming up. If I find positions in other markets that occur along the way, it's a plus. However, I could trade nothing but one market if I think there's a big move coming.

I keep moving my stops to reduce risk. I want to be in control. I'm out of control when I worry a lot. So my stops have to move up with my commitment.

Some people won't risk more than 50 percent of their margin at any one time. Do you have any rules like that?

No, I don't.

As long as your position risks no more than 5 percent of equity, you'll take a bundle of them if it's appropriate.

I'll just keep taking them, yes.

What about things like crop reports and freezes and that kind of thing? Do you take account of those as a risk management device?

Yes, depending upon the crop report and the time of the year. Unless I have a limit move under my belt, I won't be in for that report.

You'll pass a trade if it's too near a report because you think that might increase your risk?

If it's going to be a major report, one that I think will have a significant effect on the market, I will. A report to me is a gamble. If I don't have a fair amount of profit in that position by the time the report comes out, I'm gambling. I don't like to gamble. If I think the market could move enough to let me get some closed profits under my belt so I could sit through the report, I may get into the market before the report.

I don't like to hold a position through a report unless I have profits. I like to build up a cushion so that if the report goes against my position I am protected.

What about the seasonal risk of going short orange juice in the winter? Do you stay away from that?

I don't trade orange juice. I don't trade cocoa. I don't trade coffee. I don't trade plywood. I don't trade lumber. I don't trade markets that are thin or have little commercial interest because you lose control. You don't have control in those markets. They have rules on the floor at the orange juice exchange that I never heard of until they took my money.

From my own orange juice experience, I know what you are talking about. My next question was going to be, Do you ignore some markets as a risk management tool? You have already given some you don't trade. Are there others?

Those are generally the ones. I trade cotton very sparingly. I like large, liquid markets. I will on occasion trade cotton, coffee, or cocoa but very seldom. I will not trade lumber. I will not trade really thin markets. I won't trade pork bellies ever on a bet. It's too thin.

You will trade cattle?

Yes.

Hogs?

I trade hogs. I've made money in cattle and hogs. I lost a small fortune in bellies. I decided they're not my market.

What about stock indexes? Are they too big for you?

I like them intraday or option wise.

What are your favorite markets?

My favorite market is soybeans. I like the S&P and bonds.

Gold?

Yes, I like gold. I like silver. At the right time of the year I like copper.

Is that because those markets tend to cooperate well with your cycle approach?

Yes. That's because with the cycle approach and my seasonal approach I can set up times of the year when things look really good.

Are there any other risk management considerations we've left out?

Balance is the most important risk management consideration. I learned this from one of the most successful traders I know. He's a gentleman that had traded for 30 years and lost money. He came to a cycles seminar in the early 1970s. Cycles were the glue that put all his techniques together. After that he was taking millions of dollars a year out of the markets. I learned a great deal from watching him and his quest to be balanced.

If you're out of balance, you're going to make bad decisions, and trading the market is a decision game. If you're overtrading, you're out of balance. If you're overcommitted, you're out of balance. If your dollar risk is too high, you're out of balance. If you're hung over, you're out of balance. If you're sick, you're out of balance. If you need the money, you're out of balance. If you make too much money, you're out of balance. You've got to take time off. You can't trade every day. Being balanced is a major consideration that every trader should put on his wall.

How long have you been trading?

About 25 years.

Steve Briese

Steve Briese is editor of the *Bullish Review* newsletter and co-author of several computerized system programs, *Cross-Current* and *Private $tock.*

Steve, how important is managing risk in your trading?

Managing risk is the whole ball game. If you have a trading system that will catch the trend length you're trading in exchange for a reasonable risk of loss, you're going to come out ahead if you don't overtrade.

Overtrading is a word that has several meanings. Overtrading can mean too large a position in one market for an account size. Overtrading can also be trading too many markets for an account size.

I take a bottom-line approach that the risk on an individual trade should never exceed 2 percent of the account. The risk on all the open positions together should never exceed 10 percent of the account.

Trading is really a game of odds, and you need to have enough capital to withstand the runs of losses that are going to occur with any system. You do that by limiting the potential loss on each trade as well as the potential total loss at any one point.

You start by determining the trend length you're going to trade. Based on that trend length, you define the entry point at which that trend will establish itself. You then ascertain where you will have to place your stop-loss order based on where that trend will have reversed. If the difference between the entry and exit is between 1 to 2 percent of your account, you go. If it's not, you either pass on the trade or establish an entry point that keeps the risk under 2 percent of the account. You do not adjust the stop-loss point.

Every trade must have a stop-loss. If your trading system is 50 percent accurate, your price objective must be at least equal to your loss plus commission and slippage. Realistically, it's got to be higher than that in order to do better than breaking even. That's why it's terribly important to have a price objective with every trade and to exit at least a portion of your trade at that price objective.

It's just mathematics. You can objectively determine whether the system or methodology you're trading has a mathematical chance of coming out ahead. You can calculate the objectives based on historic system results. You can look and see what the average stop has been and what the average loss has been and what the number of winning trades was. You can make some systems more profitable, particularly breakout systems that are not that pretty on paper, by anticipating and entering early. You do this by using some outside indicator or simply adjusting your entry.

What kind of runs of losses should people be prepared to expect? You've done a lot of system research. How many losses in a row are common?

I think you should be ready for five.

At least five.

If you've got a system that has had more than five in a row, I would have a very difficult time being comfortable with it. I don't think you'll get five very often, but I think you should be prepared for five.

If you have a 50 percent accurate system, that's unusually good for a non–curve-fitted system with larger profits than losses. Flipping a

coin has the same probability. If you flip a coin, how long will it take to have more than five heads in a row? Not too long. So isn't five too low a number?

Yes, you can consider it a low number. But stop and think about actually trading a system. My experience with people who have bought trading systems from me is that they're not going to stay with a system that has more than five losses in a row. They are not going to be very happy with one that stops at five. It's going to be real tough. I know myself if I had a methodology that lost five times, that's when I'd start to look and see whether the current results are in line with historical results based on my hypothetical testing. I wouldn't want to lose any more than that before I started checking.

Do you have a number for the relationship between average profit and average loss that you think is a good one?

The problem there is that it would vary widely with the trend length that you're following. I've seen a lot of very short-term systems where the transaction costs are huge. With one of those you would need a much higher ratio of profit to loss. With a longer-term system, the transaction costs are small. If you have three to one, you're okay. You're going to have a nice system. Any time I see a short-term system that's showing profits of $40 a trade, I know that there are any number of brokerage houses that can eat that up for you through slippage and commissions. With something like that I don't think you can calculate a high enough profit-to-loss ratio.

If you have a reasonable system of an intermediate-term nature that trades maybe a couple of times a month, then three to one is a reasonable number. If you're trading more frequently where your transaction costs have a chance of killing you, then the sky's the limit.

Do you choose markets to trade or not to trade as a method of risk management?

Yes. I never kick myself for missing a weather move in orange juice or heating oil or one of the lumber moves. Those are the kinds of markets that are so thin they can trade limit up and limit down the same day or lock limit several days.

When the volatility gets too high, regardless of your system, there comes a point where you just have to get out. I learned this back in 1973. My first trading campaign was in silver. I bought it at $2.97 and I kept buying it all the way up to about $3.60. I thought that was about as far as it was going for the time being, so I got out.

Then I decided, "Well hell, I might as well make a little money on the reaction," so I went short. Of course, I used my accumulated profits to go short three times as much as I had been long. I was right at first. The market did go down, and I had $1,500 profit per contract. All of a sudden, the next four days the market went locked limit up. I was stuck in a position against the trend in a very volatile situation. I lost twice my commodity investment.

It's amazing that you ever came back to trade again.

People who lose big in commodities see that if they had just done the opposite, they would have won big. That's what brings them back. It certainly piqued my interest, and I've been fascinated ever since.

What markets do you disqualify for trading because of excessive risk?

I don't trade orange juice. There are a lot of markets I don't even consider.

For risk management reasons, not just because you don't like them.

Orange juice would be one.

Because of low liquidity?

Yes.

And freeze season?

Yes. I don't trade lumber because of the thinness of trading and the volatility when you get into a move. I don't trade heating oil because it is so subject to weather moves. If I trade energy, I'd rather trade gasoline or crude oil.

I don't trade cattle only because there are so few times in a decade that you can make money trading cattle, at least using my methods.

How about pork bellies?

I love pork bellies. With pork bellies and hogs the only reason I trade them is because the Commitments of Traders data are an exceptional indicator of those markets for major and intermediate-term moves. It's phenomenal. I got buy signals in both markets three days ahead of the Hog and Pig Report last June, and there was a tremendous move. That's typical. It used to be by the time you received the commitments data, it was too late in those two markets. The move had already taken place. Now we're getting the report within three days, and it's timely.

Since your maximum loss is $500, that pretty much disqualifies the S&P, doesn't it?

I consider the S&P a different animal entirely than the rest of the futures markets. I use completely different trading methods on it. I can trade the NYFE with a $500 stop-loss without any problem, but you have to be willing to take more than $500 losses to trade the S&P unless you're a day trader.

Are you saying you're willing to take more than $500 losses or that you don't trade it?

Yes, I trade it with larger stops.

Apparently you're not afraid of reports because you just talked about buying ahead of a pig crop report because of Commitments of Traders numbers.

Some of my best trades I have placed ahead of reports. I just gave an example in hogs and bellies. The 1992 bottom in the grains was before a crop report. I got buy signals in those grains from commitments data three whole weeks ahead of that report. What I like to fasten on when I start seeing signals is what is going to trigger the actual move. One of my favorite triggers is reports. In 1992, I predicted that the bottom would be the day of that report. I also predicted it would be a major bottom, and it was. The actual bottom was the day before the report. If I have strong evidence from smart money that the report is going to move the market, I love to trade ahead of reports.

Phyllis Kahn

Phyllis Kahn is the editor of *Gann Angles*. She uses Gann methods to attempt to predict turning points in advance.

Phyllis, is risk management important in your trading style?

I've already discussed risk management in the context of cutting losses short and letting profits run. You can't separate it from protective stops, both initial stop and trailing stops to protect profits. I don't have any complicated methods for it.

So your primary ingredients of risk management are to have a stop in the market at all times, to have a stop that's comfortable for you, and then to trail a stop to protect profits.

Absolutely.

Relating your risk to your equity is not that important to you, is it?

No, because I tend to undertrade rather than overtrade.

For instance, you wouldn't worry about how many positions you have on in relation to your account size?

I wouldn't say that.

Do you have some limit on the number of markets you can trade at once in relation to your account size?

Absolutely.

How do you determine that?

Very conservatively. The methods I use generate many more trades than

I can possibly take. I focus on the most heavily traded markets where you get good fills. I don't trade in thin markets like lumber and orange juice. Although the trading signals are valid, I don't feel comfortable trading thin markets. I limit my trading to four or five markets.

Which are those?

The S&P, T-bonds, silver, gold, and the grains. Occasionally, when I have a really good signal, I trade in cotton, copper, or platinum. I don't do them all at the same time. Five markets at one time is about as much as I can handle. Of course, it's related to the amount of equity in the account.

You didn't mention any currencies. Why don't you trade currencies?

I do trade them occasionally. I tend to get out of currency trades very quickly because they have such huge daily trading ranges. I take most of the Gann timer trades that I see in the currencies, but I'm out of them in a day or two. I guess fear plays a part in the currency markets, but the trades can be really good. I'm afraid to stay too long because they tend to have a huge day in one direction, closing on the high, and then open in the opposite direction with a large gap. I must be getting old; I don't enjoy that kind of volatility.

Do you have any rule of thumb as to how much of your equity you will risk in terms of margin or stop size?

Yes, absolutely. Because of the methods I use for entering the market, I always have a very limited risk on entry. Thus, most of the open trades that I would have at any time would likely be on the plus side rather than the minus side. I would have already been stopped out on the trades that weren't going to work. It's a matter of how to handle the winning trades. I don't think I would ever have more than a 20 percent overall risk for all my participation in all markets.

You keep your trailing stops to the point where you risk losing no more than 20 percent of your open profits?

Right. I'd rather be stopped out. If I'm holding positions in all five markets that I actively trade, I would be more inclined to keep the stops close when they're substantially profitable. I don't want to give those profits back.

What about things like crop reports? Do you worry about those?

I do not. My experience has been that the reports tend to come out in line with whatever the market is doing. When they don't, I have stops in and I'm stopped out. I don't let them affect my decisions at all.

Is diversification at all important to you? Do you try to pick new positions that are diverse from the ones you have?

Not really. The quality of the trade is the most important thing. What do I mean by the quality of the trade? It is a confluence of cycles from major highs and lows that creates my timing indicator.

Glen Ring

Glen Ring is editor of the *Trends in Futures* newsletter.

How important is managing risk to you?

Managing risk is in many ways the foundation of the entire process. Managing risk comes down to two things. First is how you are going to place your stops. That goes back to cutting your losses short. Define a method for managing your stops. Define a method so you have a degree of consistency in your trading. The second thing that's even more important is to have a global plan. I find that winning traders, myself included, may treat their trading like a game, but they also look at the whole thing as a money-making business.

Consider trading as a business venture. Managing risk means recognizing what the costs of trading are. Make a comprehensive plan. Keep detailed records. Define what your overall risk is. In other words, how much equity do you have to trade? How much of that equity are you willing to risk overall? Use that number to define how much risk you can accept on a given trade. Find out for a potential trade idea what your risk is and match the two up.

Either you're within your risk tolerance on the overall business plan or you're not. If you are, you take the trade. If you're not, you don't.

The insurance industry uses the statement, "Losers don't plan to fail; they fail to plan." That applies very much to the trading business, too. If you don't adequately prepare, if you don't do the planning, it's like taking a peewee football team out to play the Dallas Cowboys.

Most people think of trading as more of a performance sport than a serious business. Those that are winners at some point have incorporated the aspect of it being a serious business. If you run a business, you're going to manage risk. You do that by planning.

Do you have a rule of thumb about how much of your equity you'll risk at one time? How many positions will you put on at one time?

I really don't worry about that because I've never run into the situation yet where I've exceeded what I consider tolerable. I do have a rule of thumb in a sense. Ideally, I want to risk 1 percent of my equity on any given trade. I don't want to risk more than 5 percent in any given complex. Other than that, I haven't run into the situation because most of the time if you're willing to keep your risk to 1 to 2 percent on any given trade, that will take care of your overall risk.

You can't find enough good opportunities to bury you too deep?

That's right. It goes back to the idea of playing defense. If I don't let the opponent (in other words, the losses in my account) run up the score, I'll still be there to play the next day, next week, next month, and next year.

What about selecting markets as a means of risk management? Do you eliminate some markets for risk management reasons?

In some situations I will because of liquidity, but not too often. Realistically, what will happen is these markets will eliminate themselves. By defining the stop-loss point, the market will eliminate itself. It hasn't become much of an issue.

Is there any market on the board that I would not trade? The answer is no, not if the right situation comes along. Is there any market on the board that I haven't traded in years? The answer is yes. There are several I haven't traded, but it's because I haven't seen an opportunity that fits my parameters.

Some people would say, "No, I don't trade lumber because the liquidity is too low and I get bad fills." But that doesn't bother you?

No. Ask "Market Wizard" Ed Secota about lumber. At a trader's conference a year ago he told about how the NFA called him because they were concerned about his limit position in lumber. His answer was, "I thanked them for their concern." That was just before it took off. He had a limit long position in lumber when the market was at 130. Those that make money go where the opportunities are.

The importance of bad fills is inversely proportional to your trading time frame. My personal time frame is long term. I'm looking for one to three good opportunities in most markets in a given year. I'm going to be in those trades anywhere from a few weeks to as much as five or six months at a time. I'm trying to generate 40 to 60 trades a year. I don't have to be too concerned with a few bad fills. To somebody who is day trading or getting in and out in two or three days, skids and transaction costs become much more of an issue.

What about situational risk, such things as crop reports and freeze seasons? Do you worry about those?

I would be untruthful if I said I'm never aware of them or never pay attention to them, but effectively, no, I don't. If my methodology says be in, I'm in. I believe what people say about technical analysis. It is supposed to account for what's going on in the marketplace. Markets somehow position themselves for the big payoffs from the reports.

The one thing I hate to do is try to pick a top or bottom in conjunction with a report. If I'm trying to do that, I'm trying to pick against what has been the most recent trend. I would rather, if I'm trying to pick a top or bottom in conjunction with a report, fade the report. In other words, I'd like to do it right after the report rather than right before the report. If a person is a report-following person, the more tradeable opportunities are the ones that come after the report rather than before it. It can be the perfect catalyst for the birth of a move in the opposite direction from the market's first reaction to the report.

A great example of that is those people who watch Cattle on Feed Reports. The Cattle on Feed Reports are notorious for having the market close opposite the report within a day or two. If the report is bullish, cattle almost invariably closes down either the next day or the following day. There are exceptions. I remember in particular a Cattle on Feed Report in 1986 or 1987 that caused the market to gap up. It was a breakaway rather than a reversal. I don't think we've gone back to fill the gap yet. That was an instance where the report was the catalyst for the birth of a move in the direction the report suggested.

Reports are not a big issue with me. I often find out about a report within minutes because someone calls me to ask what I think about the report. My answer is, "What report?" I don't keep a calendar of reports, and I don't pay much attention to them.

What about diversification as a risk management tool? Do you try to diversify?

Yes, I do. There are two particular ways that I pay attention to diversification. One is by trading across a broad cross section of markets. I watch almost 40 markets, and wherever opportunity comes, I'll take it, while limiting my exposure in a given complex as I stated earlier.

The other way I diversify is by trading with several different methodologies. That will reduce the risk of getting caught in a nontrending year like 1989. It limits your profits a little bit in a heavily trending year, but it will also protect against big drawdowns. The way I do this is by looking at some trading-range methodologies. Some may call them top and bottom picking. What I call them is reacting to the market as soon as it tells me a top or bottom has occurred. I don't recommend most people trade those kind of methods until they have learned their discipline, their money management rules, and until they define very well what is an opportunity in those situations.

If people want to find the foundation for putting all this together, they'll see it every morning when they look in the mirror. It comes back to a person being able to follow his rules. Even when you establish your rules, if you can't follow them, it isn't going to work. Most people should define simpler rules rather than complex rules because we're more likely to follow a simple rule than a complex one. That's the key to managing risk and managing the entire trading process.

Jake Bernstein

Jake Bernstein has written 27 trading books and has published his weekly market letter for over 20 years.

Jake, how important is managing risk to your trading style?

Most of what I think is important about managing risk would come under cutting losses short. Another important aspect of managing risk is to trade a balanced portfolio. Don't focus all your energies on one particular market. Trade a portfolio of anywhere from 6 to 15 markets that are not closely correlated. Diversification intrinsically helps you manage risk.

Do you have a limit on how much of your account you want to commit in terms of either loss or margin or some such measure?

There's nothing wrong with a rule that limits individual losses to a certain percent of your account size, such as 1 to 5 percent.

I'm talking more about how many positions you'll have on at once.

It's important to have a buffer. If you have a $20,000 account, trade roughly half of it in margin. Let's say you have a $20,000 account. You're trading 10 and keeping 10 in reserve. With the exception of the S&P, the usual margin is about $1,500 to $2,000 per position. That means there are about five positions you can trade.

What about choosing markets and not trading some markets as a risk management tool? Do you eliminate some markets from consideration because of risk management?

Yes. One thing that never ceases to amaze me, especially in the last 10 years, is this fascination traders have with the S&P. It's a wonderful market. It moves, and it trades with big dollars per tick. Nevertheless, the vast majority of trading systems don't work in the S&P. Traders keep wanting to trade it even if they don't have the capital. If they don't have the capital, they say, "Well, if my account is too small to hold positions overnight, I'll day trade it." Most people should not be trading the S&P. They are unlikely to be successful.

You have to eliminate some markets by virtue of their nature. You can eliminate some markets because they're not conducive to trading. They're too thin. They're hard to get into and out of with decent price fills.

What markets are those?

I'm talking about markets where you really don't want to use market orders. For instance, the other day the palladium market ticked only seven times. Look at lumber. In the last few months it has been limit up or limit down almost every other day. Most people can't take that kind of heat.

Do you have a liquidity minimum, so much volume or open interest, that you require before you'll trade a market?

I like to see at least 1,500 tick-volume ticks a day.

What about situational risk like crop reports and freeze seasons? Do you pay any attention to those?

No. I used to when I was younger, but nowadays I believe my methodology is enough to keep me out of trouble. It should keep me on the correct side of the market when most of those reports come out.

Certainly, if I were day trading and I knew, for example, that later this week the Federal Reserve was meeting to make a judgment about interest rates, I would pay attention. From the standpoint of a day trader going into that day, you would expect increased volatility. You could anticipate that your trading system might not work on such a day. So you would make a decision ahead of time, "I'm not going to trade on that day."

Because it becomes more of a gamble than an intelligent trade?

Exactly. Can I just slip something in here about the European markets?

Sure.

I don't think most traders are aware of the European markets, especially the ones at the LIFFE Exchange and the Matif in Paris. They are really good markets. When I say really good, I mean it. They have very consistent trends with few interruptions. They seem to work well technically with many traditional timing indicators. The chart patterns are good. There's a lot of liquidity.

There are two negatives to trading those markets. First, the trading hours are not convenient, and second, in order to calculate how much money you've made or lost, you must also consider the currency exchange rate.

Nevertheless, some of those European markets offer great opportunities for trend followers. If you take a look at them, their trends have been absolutely beautiful. Whether they'll continue that way, I don't know. But I think they have been easier to trade than the U.S. markets.

As a practical matter do you trade them the same? Does a broker trade them the same way as the U.S. markets?

I'll give you an example. Today the Italian bond market opened at 109.85, had a high of 109.90, a low of 108.50, and closed at 109.78. Just pick up the phone and give your broker an order. It's really that simple.

Do they charge the same commission?

The commissions are higher.

How much higher?

It depends on where you trade. I'd say probably 20 to 40 percent higher, but that's negotiable.

How is the currency exchange handled? Is there a separate charge to convert back and forth?

It's all converted back and forth automatically.

So your profit appears in your account as U.S. dollars.

Correct. I'll cite you another example. The German Bund, which is the German interest rate future traded at the LIFFE, was at 101.21 back in January. It moved down to a low on March 2nd of 93.55. That's a huge move in terms of dollars. I'm not sure exactly what it was, but it was definitely in the tens of thousands of dollars.

That move was picture perfect in terms of almost all the indicators. They topped at the right time. They bottomed at the right time. They gave signals to add to the short position at the right time. The volatility was reasonable enough so you wouldn't have been knocked out of your position by dramatic bear market rallies. The size of the move was tradeable. Everything about that move was picture perfect.

Many of the ingredients of success or failure have to do with the type of markets you trade. Better trending markets make it easier for you to follow the trend and let your profits run.

The fewer reactions you have, the better it is. Are there historical price data available to use for testing?

There are some historical price data available.

Where?

They are available from the LIFFE Exchange itself. They have been very aggressive in seeking out new business and very helpful in providing data to people who want to back-test.

Do they give it to you on a computer disk?

Yes. They recently sent out a flyer to CTAs asking if they wanted data on certain contracts. All you had to do was send back the card, and they sent you a disk. I don't know if they still do that.

The trends are just fabulous. It's no wonder quite a few money managers have started actively trading those markets in preference to U.S. markets.

Tom Aspray

Tom Aspray was a pioneer in computerized technical analysis. His current area of concentration is foreign currency trading, especially in the cash market.

Tom, how important is managing risk to your style of trading?

Quite important. I've taught for many years both here in the United States and overseas. I've trained many foreign exchange dealers, and sometimes they don't manage risk as well as other professionals.

I look at the reward/risk ratio on a given trade. At a minimum I look for a three-to-one ratio. If I am correct, I want to have the potential to make three or four times as much as my initial risk. This is true whether I'm looking at a two- to three-day, two- to three-week, or two- to three-month move.

Obviously, no matter how you trade you're going to take some losses. But those big hits are what spell doom for most traders. That includes both the public and institutional traders. I've reviewed the books of traders at banks. Often, if they could cut out the one or two trades per month where they were stubborn and didn't manage their risk or went into a trade without any clear-cut exit parameters, they would perform much better.

What about the size of your positions as a percentage of your total equity? Do you look at that at all?

Yes, I do, but I don't tie it to a fixed percentage of the account. I trade mostly in the cash markets. My normal size position is about one-fifth of what I have the capability to trade. My risk based on my initial stop is a fairly small percentage of available capital. However, I don't really tie it to a specific number.

How does margin work in the cash market?

It depends on your bank. You usually pay 5 to 10 percent margin.

So it's like futures?

Yes, it's very similar to futures. There are differences in how you can use stops because you're looking at the bid and asked. It's a very liquid market in the currencies that trade 24 hours a day.

Do you think it's important to stand aside during especially risky time periods?

Clearly.

What kinds of periods are those?

My technical signals are less reliable going into an economic report. Say I put on a position during Asian trading and carry it into late European trading before the New York opening. If there's an economic report coming out and my position hasn't really performed or my signals are not strong, I generally won't take the gamble and ride it through the report. I'll cut it out.

If everyone was prohibited from trading at least 50 percent of the time, their performance would be much better. Anyone who's traded has gotten into the position where you put on a position and a day later you think what an idiot you were. You should have been doing something else. Playing golf perhaps. We all have a tendency to overtrade. The more filters you use to figure out why you shouldn't take a trade, the better off your performance will probably be.

Do you stay away from certain markets because they're too risky?

I trade mostly in the cash currency markets. The more liquid the market, the higher degree of success you're likely to have. The S&P is a market most people should avoid. Many large money managers rarely trade the S&P. Although it's the glamour market, I've seen too many people burn up trading the S&P.

Are there any other risk management techniques you use?

Perhaps an obscure or oblique risk management technique is updating my charts by hand. That allows you to get a better feel for the risk. Having to plot something manually makes you more fully confront what the market does to your position every day.

Michael Chisholm

Michael Chisholm is editor of *Taurus*, now in its 20th year of publication.

Michael, how important is risk management to trading success?

It's really important for all traders, small or big. Some of the big traders I've had occasion to talk to have more difficulty managing risk than the small traders. I've noticed over the years that when my account has been small for whatever reason, I have been really careful with it. I watch it like a hawk. When my account gets rich, I tend to fall into a habit of neglect. I'm making money. I have profits, and I'm more comfortable. I don't keep as close an eye on it. That's very foolish.

How do you handle managing risk?

I limit initial risk on any trade to no more than 5 percent of what I have available. In testing I search for those commodities that work best with my methodology and that permit reasonable initial risk.

Right now I have a portfolio of 12 commodities that I follow for my own account. I believe most traders would be best served if they constructed their own fixed portfolio and stayed with it. It's tempting to vary from your portfolio.

Let's say a trader has 12 commodities that historical testing and real-time trading have shown will work best for him. Then all of a sudden he happens to notice news stories that suggest orange juice is going to run wild. Orange juice isn't one of his 12 commodities. If my account is on the plus side, I might go ahead and take a chance on it for one or two contracts, but I won't trade it heavily. I try to resist that kind of thing because I believe discipline is important if we're going to be successful as traders. I try to stay with my basic portfolio whenever possible.

In the past, as profits mounted I might have added two or three new commodities to trade. Then I would move into my second tier of profitable commodities, those that weren't quite as good as my top portfolio. In hindsight, I no longer consider that a correct approach. What I do now instead is increase the number of contracts I trade per commodity in the same portfolio.

Another thing that is important for all traders is to diversify among commodities and complexes. I try to have a grain, a meat, a couple of foods, a petroleum, currencies, and financials—a broad spectrum. I know there are people out there who trade nothing but the grains or nothing but the meats. If a person concentrates on one complex, I suppose it enables him to become more expert in that particular area. But so often one false signal can affect the whole complex and a person can be badly hurt.

Of course, there may be a correlation between bonds and stock indexes or currencies and metals, but I believe you're less likely to suffer large drawdowns if you are spread between different complexes and different commodities. I try to achieve as much diversification as I possibly can.

An important psychological aspect of money management is knowing when to take profits out of your account. You should spend some profits rather than letting the money stay in your account indefinitely. That's been important to me over the years. I withdraw money from time to time and take a vacation or buy a new car. From a behaviorist's standpoint [Michael is a trained psychologist], it gives a sense of reward. It provides conscious and subconscious motivation.

Concerning the 12 markets you picked for your portfolio, how did you decide to cut it off at 12? Is there something magic about the number 12 for a portfolio size?

I just picked that number out. When my account size has been small for one reason or another, such as withdrawing money to pay taxes, I might have used an eight-market portfolio. At other times I've had up to 14.

The number you pick has some relationship to your account size. What's the formula you use to determine it?

It's a seat-of-the-pants kind of thing. I look at how much money I have, the margins involved, and what the average historical risk has been for a certain commodity over the years.

Is drawdown the historical risk?

Yes. I don't have a set formula for it. I play with the numbers until I come up with what seems to be an appropriate mix.

Do you eliminate any commodities from consideration for risk purposes?

The S&P. The only way I know to trade the S&P with my methodology is with stops about $10,000 away from the initial entry point. I also pass on coffee.

Why?

Over the past 10 years my methodology has shown a disproportionately high dollar risk for the potential profit.

Is that because you have to put your stops too far away, like in the S&P?

Yes. It's also because of the market's thinness and the volatility that results from that and the fundamental uncertainties. Cocoa does not work well using my methodology.

That's not a risk management reason. That's a performance reason.

Correct.

What about orange juice? Are you willing to trade orange juice? Some people don't like it.

Yes, I do trade orange juice. It's been good to me over the years. For some reason my system seems to like orange juice, and orange juice seems to like my system.

What about lumber?

I used to trade lumber, but I haven't traded it now for about a year for both risk and performance reasons.

What about situational risk like crop reports and freeze seasons? Do you ever pay attention to those?

Not except psychologically. I've looked at some of my past trades that have occurred around reports, and what I've found is that as often as not the report has benefited my position. So while I may wince knowing that an upcoming report could slice me to pieces, I trade my system mechanically regardless of reports.

Are you reluctant to go short orange juice during freeze season or do you just go with your system?

I go with the system. I have confidence that my system will pick up and reflect the fundamentals accurately.

Bob Jubb

Bob Jubb is editor of *Tomorrow's Commodities,* one of the few advisory services that operates without a hotline.

How important is managing risk in your trading style?

It's the key. That's how you keep your confidence up and maintain your potential to trade. If you lose your nest egg, you can't trade any more. If you lose 50 percent right away, you will have destroyed your confidence. You might as well quit right then. You have to stay around until you catch some luck in the form of a big move.

If you go after at least $2 in profit for every $1 you're going to risk and you can bat anywhere near 50 percent and your reward of $2 comes out periodically, you will make money. You'll be among those 10 percent of traders who make money versus the 90 percent who don't.

If you can't manage your risk, you won't be around long. If you have a $10,000 account and you short coffee before one of its big runs and you forget to get out, you will lose your $10,000 in one trade. Managing risk is the defense of the game. The offense is letting your profits run. Part of managing risk is using stops and cutting your losses short.

You have previously recommended risking $1,000 per trade on a $10,000 account. If you had a $20,000 account instead of a $10,000 account, would you still trade one contract and risk $1,000 or would you trade two contracts now?

I would trade two and risk $1,000 on each.

You're comfortable risking 10 percent on one trade?

Right.

And you're not worried about a string of seven losses in a row.

No. I've only had that happen twice in 20 years. When it happens it's very unfortunate. But something that happens 10 percent of the time, you can't worry about. Twice in 20 years is 10 percent. I never worry about seven in a row. I'm not saying it won't happen again. I'll be publishing 10 more years and it will probably happen during the next 10 years. It's not something I am going to worry about.

So your principle method of managing risk is to risk no more than $1,000 on each trade and always attempt to achieve at least a $2,000 profit.

When I'm writing the letter and can't find a trade like that, I look for my favorite trade and set an entry point that will create the $2,000 profit. About two or three times a year I end up in that situation and have to buy something with a limit order.

What about diversification as a risk management tool? How do you look at that? If you have a grain and a metal on and are looking for a new trade, do you try to avoid the grains and the metals?

Yes. There are some areas I'm more confident about. I'm much more confident in grains than meats. If I already have a grain though, I'll take my favorite meat trade instead. If I have meats, grains, coffee, and sugar, I won't look at cocoa or cotton. There are many markets that influence each other. I try to make sure I'm not involved in too many related markets that will all go down together or all explode if we happen to be short.

So diversification is very important to you.

Oh, yes. It's like the current fad where people are taking all their money from CDs and putting it in mutual funds. If the stock market ever starts down, I'll want to short it because there will be panic selling I'm afraid.

What about situational risk like crop reports and freeze seasons? Do you worry about those things increasing your risk or do you ignore them?

No. I pay attention to when they're going to occur. I make an estimate of what they could and couldn't do to me. If I'm really nervous about one, I'll tighten my stop. Or if I'm considering putting on a second contract, I will rarely do it in front of a report because if I'm wrong I've just doubled my exposure. That goes with my conservative approach. But I don't run from them.

What about avoiding markets altogether because you think they're too risky? Which ones would those be?

Some because they're too risky. There are some markets I do not understand and don't have the inclination to. I figure why look at European bonds when you can trade U.S. bonds. Some markets I like but avoid just because there isn't enough activity during certain periods of the year: orange juice sometimes, lumber sometimes.

I've started to look at the rice market. I haven't made any trades yet. I'm watching the chart, trying to get a feel for it. I'm going to call and get some material just to start learning about a new area. With China coming on strong, rice is going to become a market that people will slowly trade more and more.

Do you look at open interest, volume?

Both.

What's your threshold for liquidity?

That's a good question. I don't have any specific requirements. I look at each market in light of what I remember from the year before.

Jack Schwager

Jack Schwager is director of futures research and trading strategy at Prudential Securities, Inc. He is also a coprincipal of Wizard Trading, a commodity money management firm and the author of *Market Wizards* and *The New Market Wizards*.

Jack, how important is risk management in your trading?

Managing risk is very similar to cutting losses. It's essential that you do that, otherwise you're doomed to fail. Everybody will eventually be wrong, and if you have no way of managing risk, one dead wrong call can wipe out an account.

You need some sort of strategy. Managing risk is not just a matter of limiting your loss on each trade. It's also using leverage in a way that is consistent with limiting drawdowns to what you consider a liveable range. You must avoid overtrading, which is also a common mistake for most novices.

The way you trade a large account is through massive diversification of everything—systems and markets. Correct?

Massive diversification would be the way to put it.

For a smaller account that can't do that, how about diversification in markets as a method of managing risk? Is that important?

Yes. There are varying schools on diversification. I come from the school that says the more the better. There are people who disagree with that. For a small account the idea is to diversify across as many markets as possible.

What about managing risk by saying you won't trade certain markets because they're inherently too risky?

Yes, that's true. If the account is large enough, you want to trade everything unless for some reason you develop a methodology that you believe doesn't work on some markets. That's an exception.

The other case is a smaller trader who doesn't have enough capital to trade some markets. It's not a matter of avoiding the market because it's too volatile. It's a matter of being unable to trade the market because the closest meaningful stop point would result in a loss that far exceeds prudent risk boundaries. For example, the S&P is a fairly volatile contract. I would consider 300 points a minimal stop in the S&P for almost any approach. That's $1,500 and a close stop at that. For people whose accounts really can't stand more than a $750 to a $1,000 loss on any given trade, you can't trade the S&P. It's too big for the person's risk tolerance.

What about a market that's illiquid? Doesn't that make it more risky and maybe a good reason not to trade it?

For most people that's not a factor because an individual trading a couple of contracts isn't going to make a difference. Almost any market is liquid enough unless it's one of those markets that is hardly trading. Even in lumber it's not a factor. If you're trading $50 million or something like that, then lumber is going to be too thin to trade. But to the individual trader, it's not going to make a difference.

Even if the open interest is less than 3,000 contracts, for a one-contract trader that's not a problem?

I don't think so. As long as you have average volume of 500 contracts a day, you probably can get by with one- or two-contract orders. If you're trying to trade 100 contracts at a clip, then it's a problem.

What about the maximum position you'll have on or the maximum number of positions you'll have on in relation to your account size? Is that important to managing risk?

I think it is, but I don't think it should be measured with maximum numbers. It needs to be measured in terms of some sort of risk measurement. In other words, you shouldn't say you're going to trade four T-bond contracts maximum in the account. You may want to trade four T-bonds depending on the market situation. If the market is much more volatile, you might want to limit yourself to two. If the market is much less volatile, you might trade eight. So you want to have some standard number, but that number should be variable depending upon the volatility of the market.

Some people say they don't want to trade any more than 50 percent of their account in margin at any one time.

Margin is a very crude way of measuring risk. I would not use margin. I would look at some measurement that directly utilizes the market's volatility, however you define that.

If, as you have said, you're risking no more than 3 percent of your account on any one trade, it's pretty hard to overtrade as long as you're trading one contract position.

Yes.

But for a guy that might be risking a higher percentage because he has a small account, he must be more careful about the total overall risk he assumes.

I agree. But margin is not as well correlated to true risk as I would like. There are much better risk measurements than margin. But not having total positions account for more than a certain percent of margin is a quick and dirty way of doing it.

What about saying you don't want to have the total dollar risk in your account greater than some percentage of the account?

That's fine. You can accumulate all your positions into a single risk management measure and have it not exceed a certain amount relative to the total size of the account.

Do you have a quick estimate of what that might be?

It depends on what measurement you're using to define risk. I don't want to reveal exactly how I do that.

What about situational risk like crop reports and freeze seasons? Should a small trader worry about those?

To some extent. You don't necessarily want to avoid having a position going into a report. In many cases that will prevent you from getting some of the best moves. What you have to know is which of those reports are particularly critical. For example, take orange juice. It's not a major market, but it is a good example of what I'm talking about.

Consider the October Crop Production Report in orange juice. In the 27 years this market has traded, 21 times we've had limit moves following that report. In many cases there have been strings of limit moves. Somebody who is not willing to risk more than a limit move would have to forgo having an orange juice position going into the October Crop Production Report. You want to know those reports that can give you the extreme moves. They should probably be avoided. A regular crop report comes with the territory. In most cases, you should be willing to assume that type of risk.

It is one thing to know the cardinal principles of trading but quite another to be able to follow them consistently. In the next chapter we'll look at the important principles of futures trading psychology.

CHAPTER 6

Psychology

Having elaborated at length on the essential ingredients of a successful trading plan, it would be a good idea to discuss the reasons why traders who have a plan nevertheless fail because they are unable to follow it.

I should start with the concept of a plan. There are very few traders who actually have any plan to begin with. Under the circumstances, whether they succeed or fail is based on luck. They have no way of knowing whether the method they may apply to any given trading decision is a profitable method. The only way to determine that is to conduct extensive historical testing or extensive testing via real-time trading. But without a plan, without rules, without specifics, there is nothing to test. There is no way to learn from mistakes because there is no way to know what constitutes a mistake.

This is not to say it is impossible to make money without a plan. A trader could be lucky and bumble along doing mostly the wrong things and some of the right things and still make impressive profits over a long period of time. That is one of the real stumbling blocks to success. The market does not always penalize you when you trade incorrectly. It does not always reward you when you trade correctly. That makes it considerably harder to learn what is correct and what is incorrect. However, eventually if you are applying losing methods, you will lose. The more you trade, the more you will lose. If you are unlucky, you will lose your precious capital very quickly.

The reason most traders don't have a plan is laziness. We all lead busy lives. We are always looking for shortcuts. Most of us don't want to work hard if we don't have to. Creating a specific, written trading plan is hard work. Testing the ideas in the plan is very hard work. It is not especially hard intellectually, but it does take time. The more you do it, the easier it becomes, but most people never bother to try in the first place. They are lazy. They hope that they can do well without too much work. This is unrealistic. Every worthwhile achievement in life requires substantial effort. There are very few overnight successes. Commodity futures trading is no different.

Another potential reason for not having a plan is that the trader does not know he needs a plan or he may not be smart enough to learn how to create a winning plan. I doubt the latter applies to most people as the concepts are not intellectually difficult. If you think it applies to you, then don't try to trade yourself. Create some approach in which you are confident, but that does not require any input from you. An example would be using a professional money manager.

Having a trading plan does not necessarily mean creating your own system from scratch. You might use someone else's trading system. I make available to my customers the trading systems and computer software I use to trade my personal capital. But even if you were going to use my systems and software, you would still have to determine how much capital to commit and what markets to trade.

Other potential reasons for not having a plan might be ego or wishful thinking. A person may know that you need a plan to succeed but think because of his brilliance, he can be the exception. Perhaps, but I doubt it. Wishful thinking is closely related to laziness. If you trade by wishful thinking, your success or failure will depend on luck.

Assuming you have a specific trading plan that will actually lead to profits if applied consistently over time, you are still not guaranteed to make those profits. The temptations are great to deviate from the plan.

One big psychological reason people deviate from their plan is the desire to gamble. I make no value judgment on this. If people want to gamble, that's up to them, but they shouldn't be surprised if they lose money. Although it appears that there is a strong flavor of gambling in the process of futures trading, most successful traders are very averse to gambling. I have talked to many who agree with me that they have no desire whatever to gamble in any context. Many commodity trading seminars take place in Las Vegas. Most successful traders can walk around in the casinos all weekend and never place a bet.

While I am not an expert in gambling psychology, I know that experts believe that compulsive gambling is often related to childhood experiences. Such gamblers often come from families with a history of compulsive gambling or alcoholism. They may have had a very critical or rejecting parent. Their gambling fever is an effort to make a big score that will show that parent, and everyone else, that they are a worthy person.

A strong desire to gamble may come from being brought up to be highly competitive. It may also come from parents who overvalued money in relation to other values as a way to achieve happiness in life. Finally, gambling may compensate for a substantial physical or developmental problem during childhood.

If any of this strikes a responsive chord, you should consider whether you are treating your trading as a giant gambling casino. If you are, don't be surprised if you don't make any money at it.

Assuming you have overcome the hurdles to creating a tested, written trading plan and you are not a gambler, what are the other reasons you will probably fail to follow your plan? At the risk of sounding trite, the two likeliest culprits are fear and greed.

The fear I am talking about is the fear of losing. This is caused by excessive risk aversion. Some of the best writing on the element of fear in trading is in Mark Douglas's book, *The Disciplined Trader* (New York Institute of Finance, 1990).

Another of my all-time favorite commodity trading quotes comes from that book. Douglas says, "Most people like to think of themselves as risk takers, but what they really want is a guaranteed outcome with some momentary suspense to make them feel as if the outcome had been in doubt. The momentary suspense adds the thrill factor necessary to keep our lives from getting too boring."

Most fear-based decisions come from the fear of losing money, although there is also the element of not wanting to be wrong. Amateur traders equate a losing trade with making a wrong (dumb) decision. Professionals understand that even the best decisions often result in losses and that you must divorce losing from ego. The real dumb decision is not following your plan regardless of the trade's result.

Fear can cause you to deviate from your trading plan in a number of ways. You can pass a trade your plan signals because you are afraid it won't work. This could be because you have a contrary opinion on the likely future direction of the market or because your system has just taken five losses in a row and you are losing confidence in it generally.

Fear can cause you to ignore or override an exit your plan signals. You can exit a trade before the plan tells you, or fail to exit when the plan dictates.

Fear of loss can cause both types of mistakes. You may hold a losing trade too long because you decide you cannot "afford" to take such a big loss as you have already incurred. (This is nonsense because you have already suffered the loss anyway, but it is the way many traders think.) You may exit a losing trade before it reaches your stop because you are afraid of a bigger loss than you currently have. You may exit a winning trade too soon because you are afraid your profit will turn into a loss.

Everyone is afraid of losing. This is a natural human emotion that you can never completely eliminate. The key is to keep it under control so it does not make you abandon your winning plan. Those who can keep fear under control are those who have the correct degree of risk aversion to trade futures. You can learn to handle the fear involved in trading through experience—the same way you learn to control other fears involved in life. If you have such a low threshold of risk aversion that fear overcomes your discipline, you will never be able to execute your plan consistently and you should not trade at all.

Another easy error to make is taking a trade not signaled by your model. The operative emotion here is greed, but the real culprit is that somehow you have developed an opinion on a situation independent of your model. You think there is a profit opportunity even though your rules tell you not to act.

It is simply a matter of ego when people think they are better than their model. Read William Eckhardt's chapter in *The New Market Wizards* by Jack Schwager (HarperBusiness, 1992). He talks about his surprise at finding out trading his system with judgment was not better than just trading his system.

This does not mean you can never modify your trading plan. But don't do it because of an opinion on a market. Do it because testing shows your new model is better than the old one.

Peter Brandt, author of *Trading Commodity Futures with Classical Chart Patterns* (Advanced Trading Seminars, 1990), is very clear about the distinction between opinions and positions. "It is our role to have positions—but not opinions," he says. Likewise, never ask someone else for an opinion. If you must ask, ask about their position.

Most experienced traders will say that the psychological aspects of trading are much more important than entries and exits. However, it is difficult to rearrange our psyches in complicated ways. So how are we to cultivate the patience and discipline needed to follow our proven, tested trading plan? One good way is to accept the reality that having opinions independent of your plan is the most destructive thing you can do.

Absent any opinions, you are free to follow your rules. That is the way to be a successful trader.

That covers the key aspects of profitable trading. Now let me summarize what you have learned.

CHAPTER 7

Summary and Conclusion

The explosion in commodity trading literature and computer software in the past 10 years has made commodity trading appear complex and difficult. The truth is good trading is a lot less complicated than it appears. You can reduce successful trading to four key principles: (1) Trade with the trend, (2) cut losses short, (3) let profits run, and (4) manage risk. Any successful trading approach will necessarily incorporate each of these principles in some way.

Note that learning to predict the markets is not one of the principles. That is the biggest mistake all new traders make. They conclude that the key to success is predicting the markets. I have news for you. The markets are not predictable. Luckily, contrary to outward appearances, you do not need to predict the markets to make money trading. I have done extremely well in each of the last five years and don't have the faintest idea where the markets are going tomorrow, next week, next month, or next year.

Mathematical analysis has shown that in most commodity markets, price action is primarily random with a small trend component. It is the trend component that allows a trader to achieve a long-term statistical edge that translates into profits. In order to exploit the trend component, however, you must trade with the trend.

Trend is only relevant in a particular time frame. To trade with the trend, you must know what your time frame is. Then you must have a method of identifying the trend in that time frame. One way to establish time frame is by the length of the price chart you use. The possibilities are intraday, daily, weekly, or monthly. Some traders combine two or more.

An important variable in selecting your time frame is the level of risk you want to assume. Generally speaking, the longer your time frame, the greater will be the necessary level of risk on each trade.

Our experts had selected a number of different time frames and had many different ways to identify the trend. Some examples are chart patterns, mathematical indicators (such as Moving Averages, Stochastics, Momentum, Directional Movement, RSI, etc.), seasonal charts, trendlines, Elliott Wave patterns, and cycles. If there was one underlying theme in their comments, it was that no matter what method you use, you should have a very precise definition of when the trend is up, down, or sideways (indeterminate).

Strictly speaking, cutting losses short is an ingredient of managing risk. It is so important to successful trading that I devoted a separate principle to it. Every successful trader understands that the decision of how to cut losses if a trade does not work out must be a key element of the trade selection process for every trade.

Our experts had numerous ways of cutting losses short. They included chart-based stops, indicator stops, entry method stops, volatility stops, money management stops, margin-based stops, and account equity stops. The method you choose will relate to your trading personality and the method you use for entering trades.

The most difficult of the various trading decisions is when to exit a profitable trade. Most aspiring traders spend almost all their time working on entry methods. This is probably because they believe that near-perfect entries can compensate for deficiencies in other areas. Since near-perfect entries are possible only in hindsight, experienced traders come around to the point where they place the least emphasis on entry.

The experts had as many different ways to let profits run as they did to cut losses short. I separated them into the following categories: trailing stops, profit targets, and reverse entry signals. The most popular was trailing stops. The trailing-stop methods were based on indicators, volatility, chart patterns, and dollar amounts. A few said letting profits run was not important to their style of trading. Others used multiple methods.

Previous commodity trading literature usually refers to the topics I group under risk management as "money management." I think risk management is a more precise description of these concepts.

There is great popular misunderstanding about the riskiness of futures trading. The truth is that trading can be just as risky as you want to make it.

While you can never control risk to the penny on each trade, you can easily determine the general level of risk over a year's time. The question is: Can you control yourself?

The most important way to control risk is by using initial protective stops. Other ways include choosing not to trade certain markets, not trading during certain dangerous time periods, limiting the number of markets and contracts traded at any one time, and trading a diversified portfolio of markets and methods. Although all the experts agreed on the general importance of risk management, they had differing opinions on the importance of each specific category. How you employ the various potential risk management alternatives will depend on your personality, trading method, and level of risk aversion.

While there are different opinions as to the proper hierarchy of the four principles, I believe there is one that is most crucial in a practical sense. In an interview for Jake Bernstein's book, *Market Masters*, when asked to choose between having discipline or a good trading system, I suggested that having the discipline to keep losses small was perhaps the most important ingredient to trading success. I said, "If a trader could do only that, he or she might stumble on enough winning trades to make some money." Many others have offered variations on the theme that if a trader can only control the losses, the profits will take care of themselves.

I recently read the following advice to traders: "Success in trading depends on two things: (1) Finding a method that matches your personal trading style, and (2) sticking to the method. It really is that simple. Almost any method will work, if it matches your personality and incorporates good money management principles."

This sounds good, but it is false. Nearly all methods suggested by the conventional wisdom do not work.

The eminent Jack Schwager does emphasize the importance of the trading style matching the personality. It is one of his principal conclusions about how to become a successful trader. In both his *Wizards* books he comments on how each Wizard found a trading style that matched his or her personality.

It is wrong to conclude from this, however, that any trading style that matches *your personality* will work. You must have both: a trading style that works and one that matches your personality. The former is clearly more important than the latter.

While accommodating your personality has a certain feel-good aspect that a trader can use to justify what he or she wants to do, I believe it is a significant

Bruce Babcock

Bruce attended Yale University and the University of California at Berkeley. He received his Bachelor's degree in Business Administration as well as a law degree. His career as a federal prosecutor included the successful prosecution of Manson family member Sandra Good in connection with the conspiracy to assassinate President Ford. He has tried many cases as defense counsel including a first degree murder case.

In 1979, at age 35, he left his law office to concentrate on commodity trading. This is his eighth commodity trading book. Other titles include *The Dow Jones-Irwin Guide to Trading Systems*, *Trendiness in the Futures Markets,* and *Profitable Commodity Trading from A to Z*. He has had numerous articles published in *Futures* and other magazines.

In April 1983, Bruce started publishing *Commodity Traders Consumer Report*. This bimonthly magazine tracks the performance of the top commodity advisory services and has made a significant impact on the industry.

In addition to all his writing on futures trading, Bruce has also designed numerous computer software programs for traders. These include 25 different optimizable trading system programs, two unique trading tools, and two data management programs for using continuous contracts.

He is one of the few system vendors who actually trades with the systems he sells. Bruce trades his personal money only with systems he also shares with the public. Between 1991 and 1995, he averaged over 50 percent annual return in his systems account. (Past performance is not necessarily indicative of future performance.)

Bruce lives in Sacramento, California. An active commodity trader himself since 1975, Bruce continues to trade the markets for his own account. His hobbies include golf and golf-club making. You can request a catalog or write to him in care of Reality Based Trading Company, 1731 Howe Avenue, Suite 149, Sacramento, CA 95825. (800)-999-2827 or (916)-677-7562. Fax (916)-672-0425. e-mail: babcock@spider.lloyd.com.

cause of trading failure. The unfortunate truth is the odds are overwhelming that the trading style that matches your personality will be a loser. How else can you explain that upwards of 95 percent of people fail at commodity trading?

The way to succeed is not to find a trading style that matches your personality, but rather to find a trading style that works. The two are almost always mutually exclusive. The methods that work are not those that make sense, feel comfortable, and are easy to implement. If they were, a lot more people would be successful.

If you want to make money at this rather than just have a good time, here are the four things you should do: Develop a proven trading model. The emphasis is on *proven*. That's your trading plan. Raise enough capital to trade it. Overcome your fear of losses. Finally, forget about having opinions on the markets. Just follow your model. That seems very doable, doesn't it? It is the essence of successful futures trading.

BIBLIOGRAPHY

The following books have been authored by the experts quoted in this book.

Alexander, Colin. *Capturing Full-Trend Profits in the Commodity Futures Markets.* Brightwaters, NY: Windsor, 1992.

Angle, Kelly. *One Hundred Million Dollars in Profits: An Anatomy of a Market Killing.* Brightwaters, NY: Windsor, 1989.

Babcock, Bruce. *The Dow Jones-Irwin Guide to Trading Systems.* Burr Ridge, IL: Dow Jones-Irwin, 1989.

————. *Profitable Commodity Futures Trading from A to Z.* Sacramento, CA: Advanced Trading Seminars, 1994.

————. *Trendiness in the Futures Markets.* Sacramento, CA: Advanced Trading Seminars, updated through 1995.

Bernstein, Jake. *Beyond the Investor's Quotient.* New York: John Wiley & Sons, 1986.

————. *The New Investor's Quotient.* New York: John Wiley & Sons. 1986.

————. *Seasonal Concepts in Futures Trading.* New York: John Wiley & Sons, 1986.

————. *Facts on Futures.* Chicago: Probus, 1987.

———— *The Handbook of Economic Cycles.* Burr Ridge, IL: Business One-Irwin, 1991

————. *Why Traders Lose—How Traders Win.* Chicago: Probus, 1992.

————. *Market Masters.* Chicago: Dearborn, 1994.

————. *Seasonal Trader's Bible.* Winnetka, IL: MBH, 1995.

Brandt, Peter. *Trading Commodity Futures with Classical Chart Patterns.* Sacramento, CA: Advanced Trading Seminars, 1990.

Bressert, Walter. *The Power of Oscillator/Cycle Combinations.* Vero Beach, FL: Bressert, 1991.

Chisholm, Michael. *Games Investors Play.* Winchester, VA: B&B, 1981.

―――. *The Taurus Method.* Brightwaters, NY: Windsor, 1983.

Schwager, Jack. *A Complete Guide to the Futures Markets.* New York: John Wiley & Sons, 1984.

―――. *Market Wizards.* New York: New York Institute of Finance, 1989.

―――. *The New Market Wizards.* New York: HarperCollins, 1992.

―――. *Schwager on Futures: Fundamental Analysis.* New York: John Wiley & Sons, 1995.

―――. *Schwager on Futures: Technical Analysis.* New York: John Wiley & Sons, 1995.

Smith, Courtney. *Profits through Seasonal Trading.* New York: John Wiley & Sons, 1980.

―――. *Commodity Spreads.* New York: John Wiley & Sons, 1981; Greenville, SC: Traders Press, 1989.

―――. *How to Make Money Trading Stock Index Futures.* New York: McGraw-Hill, 1985; paperback, 1988.

―――. *Options Strategies.* New York: John Wiley & Sons, 1987.

―――. *Seasonal Charts for Futures Traders.* New York: John Wiley & Sons, 1987.

Wasendorf, Russell. *Commodity Trading—The Essential Primer.* Burr Ridge, IL: Dow Jones-Irwin, 1984.

―――. *All About Futures.* Chicago: Probus, 1991.

―――. *All About Commodities.* Chicago: Probus, 1992.

―――. *All About Options.* Chicago: Probus, 1993.

Williams, Larry. *How I Made One Million Dollars Last Year Trading Commodities.* Brightwaters, NY: Windsor, 1974.

―――. *The Definitive Guide to Commodity Trading, Volumes One and Two.* Brightwaters, NY: Windsor, 1988 and 1989.

Williams, Larry, and Michele Noseworthy. *Sure Thing Commodity Trading.* Brightwaters, NY: Windsor, 1977.

INDEX

A-B-C pattern 35
Account equity stop 100, 107
   minimum 154
   size, in selecting time frame 5
   size, minimum 91
Accuracy, percent 76, 96
ADX 30, 31, 47, 132
ADXR 47, 132
Agri-Finance Magazine 13
Alabama Farm Bureau 89
Alexander, Colin 25, 26, 106, 113, 147
All About Commodities 57
All About Futures 57
All About Options 57
Always-in-the-market system 96
Angle, Kelly 18, 19, 97, 117, 148
Anticipating 7
APM Trend Watch 47
Aspray, Thomas 45, 46, 81, 132, 194
Aspray's Forex Trader 46
Asset allocation 45
Autopilot 6

Bad fills 189
Balance 175, 180
Baldwin, Tom 73
Bears, Chicago 75
Bernstein, Jake 9, 10, 89, 137, 190, 214
Best-fit line 8
Blood Flow Theory 119
Blowoff, trailing stop during 135
Bottom picking 129
Brandt, Peter 22, 23, 76, 130, 163, 210
Breakeven stop 116, 133
Breakout entry 7
Breakout rule, four-week 14
Breakout systems 181
Breakout trading 22

Breakouts 68
   trading 21
   volatility 63
Bressert, Walter 52, 53, 82, 120, 175
Briese, Steve 5, 7, 102, 135, 180
Bullish Review newsletter 7, 102, 135, 180
Business venture, trading as 188

Cambridge Hook 39
Canadian Society of Technical Analysts 13
Candlestick Hotline 14
Capturing Full-Trend Profits in the
Commodity Futures Markets 27
Carnell, Ginny 30
Channel entry method 138
Channel, moving average 11
Chart
   continuation 68
   continuous 68
   daily 5, 8, 21, 24, 30, 31, 45,
      59, 67, 72, 84
   formations 5
   hourly 84, 139
   intraday 67, 84, 139
   monthly 5, 24, 30, 59, 132, 134
   pattern 5, 71
   pattern targets 131
   points, trailing stop using 113
   weekly 8, 13, 24, 30, 31, 43,
      47, 59, 68, 72, 84, 132, 134
Chart-based stops 71
Chicago Bears 75
Chisholm, Michael 27, 28, 85, 115, 196
Classical chart patterns 130
Close-only stop 101, 112
CNBC cable channel 13
collusion in the pits 96
comfort, risk 153